About this book

This book is divided into five sections.

The essence of California pages 6–19
Introduction; Features; Food and Drink; Short Break including the 10 Essentials

Planning pages 20–33
Before you go; Getting there; Getting around; Being there

Best places to see pages 34–55
The unmissable highlights of any visit to California

Best things to do pages 56–73
Good places to have lunch; Best beaches; Best shopping areas; Places to take the children and more

Exploring pages 74–185
The best places to visit in California, organized by area

▼ to ▼▼▼▼ denotes AAA rating

Maps

All map references are to the maps on the covers. For example, San Jose has the reference ✚ 4J – indicating the grid square in which it is to be found

Admission prices

Entry fees at attractions are indicated by the following categories:
Inexpensive (under $10);
Moderate ($10 to $20);
Expensive (over $20)

Hotel prices

Prices are per room per night: $ budget (under $100); $$ moderate ($100–$250); $$$ expensive (over $250)

Restaurant prices

Prices are for a three-course meal per person without drinks: $ budget (under $20); $$ moderate ($20–$40); $$$ expensive (over $40)

Contents

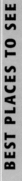

Original text by Richard Minnich
Revised and updated by Nick Edwards

© AA Media Limited 2012
First published 2008. Information revised and updated 2012
ISBN: 978-0-7495-7079-8

Published by AA Publishing, a trading name of AA Media Limited, whose registered
office is Fanum House, Basing View, Basingstoke, Hampshire RG21 4EA.
Registered number 06112600.

This book or
m. Inquiries

. Due to its
onsible for
any reliance by
consumers
ice only and
and may
Ne have tried
now if you

nave any comments at travelguides@theAA.com.

Colour separation: AA Digital Department
Printed and bound in Italy by Printer Trento S.r.l.

Find out more about AA Publishing and the wide range of services the AA provides by
visiting our website at theAA.com/shop

A04463
Maps in this title produced from mapping © MAIRDUMONT/Falk Verlag 2011
Transport map © Communicarta Ltd, UK

BEST THINGS TO DO

EXPLORING...

The essence of...

One of the best things about California is that you rarely have to plan your vacation around the seasons. If you wish to relax on the beach, accommodations range from luxurious oceanside resorts to basic camping facilities. If you want continuous entertainment, the state abounds with theme parks, fairs and festivals, as well as the myriad nightlife afforded by the main cities.

For the explorer or seeker of beauty, the natural habitat is varied and unbeatable. For a tour of the coastline, the Amtrak rail system runs from the top to the bottom of the state and features plush, picture-windowed lounge cars. The landscape is perfect for the photographer.

THE ESSENCE OF CALIFORNIA

features

The popular image of California is one of blue skies, bronzed surfers and Hollywood glamour. The reality is that and so much more. True, the southern coast offers miles of sandy beaches and a warm climate most of the year but in contrast the northern coast can be foggy and chilly, even in summer.

Inland the state offers incredible variety, from the southern deserts through thousands of acres of lush farmlands to the majesty of the Sierra Nevada and Cascade mountains. Crystal clear lakes and vast forests containing the oldest and tallest trees on earth complete a picture of geographical diversity that would do any country proud.

When you consider that California has two of the planet's most famous and vibrant cities in Los Angeles and San Francisco on top of the variety of natural splendors to be enjoyed, it's easy to realize how it has something to please everyone.

GEOGRAPHY
- Population: 37,000,000.
- Land area: 155,959sq miles (399,894sq km).
- Highest point: Mount Whitney (14,494ft/4,419m).
- Lowest point: Death Valley (282ft/86m below sea level).
- Capital: Sacramento.

DEMOGRAPHICS AND ECONOMICS

● California is equally diverse in terms of its 37 million residents. In addition to the residual Native American population and descendants of the Gold Rush era '49ers, every wave of immigrant has lapped onto its Pacific shores. The proximity of Mexico means that there is a strong Hispanic influence, visible from the venerable string of Missions to the ubiquitous presence of *taquerias*.

● Despite enormous debts brought on by the recession, the state continues to be the leading agricultural economy in the US, primarily because of its fruit crops and globally respected wine industry, while pockets of logging and fishing also remain. The movie mecca of Hollywood, hi-tech hub of Silicon Valley and statewide tourism all generate huge incomes too.

FLORA AND FAUNA

● Again diversity is the theme. The Pacific Ocean is home to humpback whales, sea otters, seals, sea lions, dolphins, elephant seals, blue whales and myriad fish species.

● On land, mammals include bison, Roosevelt elk, big-horn sheep, mountain lions, bobcats, wild burros and black bears, while the desert has its own inhabitants, such as iguanas, chuckawallas, pronghorn antelope, coyotes, kangaroo rats and various insects and reptiles, including the black widow spider and the rattlesnake.

● Birdlife ranges from the exotic white-faced ibis and the tiny hummingbird to the bald and golden eagles and various seabirds. They are spoilt for choice when it comes to perches, as California also has a huge panoply of trees. Among these are eucalyptus, sequoias, redwoods, Joshua trees and many varieties of palm. Various cacti and flowers also abound year-round.

food & drink

California's huge cultural diversity leads to a mouthwatering palette of dining possibilities. Restaurants boasting delights from every corner of the globe line the streets of the major cities, while various ethnic establishments can be found alongside American ones in even the smallest communities. Fast-food outlets are inevitably ever-present but a sizeable percentage of the population is conscious of both health and body image, so organic vegetarian options are also easy to come by. Indeed, the desire to eat wholesome local ingredients led to the state spawning its very own style of cuisine.

CALIFORNIA CUISINE

Genuine California cuisine originated in Berkeley in the 1970s, when Alice Waters started blending French-influenced recipes with fresh local produce and seasonal vegetables. Her legendary Chez Panisse restaurant is still going strong nearly four decades later, while other respected chefs such as Gary Danko and Michael Mina have also established themselves in the Bay Area and beyond.

Menus typically specify exactly where the ingredients have come from, so you may well find yourself ordering grilled and braised Magruder pork with wild mustard seed sauce, Chino Ranch savoy cabbage and roasted onions, followed by Sierra Beauty apple and walnut gallette with Cognac ice cream.

OTHER TASTES

Nearby Mexico exerts a strong influence, although Cal-Mex, as the local version is known, is lighter than Tex-Mex. Its signature flavors are due to the generous use of avocados, salsa and cilantro (coriander). Certain areas, such as San Francisco's Mission District, specialize in

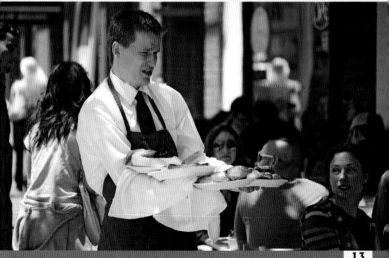

super burritos bulging with rice, beans, spicy salsa and a choice of meat.

Other areas that stand out for a particular type of cuisine are San Francisco's Chinatown for Chinese and North Beach for authentic Italian, while San Jose offers superb Vietnamese, Beverly Hills has great Jewish delis and Solvang features fine Scandinavian food. All along the coast are seafood houses to fit every budget, with fish like mahi mahi and tuna being favorites.

THE GRAPE AND THE HOP

California wineries have long been established on the global scene and many of them have scooped international awards ahead of their more traditional European rivals. Among the most famous are Mondavi, Beringer, Domaine Chandon, Buena Vista, Sebastiani and Korbel. One favorite is Mondavi's unfiltered Cabernet Sauvigon, while Pinot Noirs and Syrahs are also highly rated.

Over the last decade or two, local micro-breweries have become increasingly popular and started to produce some excellent hoppy IPAs,

ambers and nutty brown ales that put the tasteless fizzy lager of the multinational giants in the shade. Sierra Nevada, based in Chico, has even started exporting its brews, while Eureka's Lost Coast Brewery and the Anderson Valley Brewing Company have a growing reputation.

OTHER TIPPLES

The Mexican margarita is the cocktail of choice, while the martini is said to have originated in San Francisco and the Mai Tai cocktail was invented at the original location of Trader Vic's in Oakland. Of course, most bars are stocked with every sort of short you can imagine.

short break

If you only have a short time to visit California and would like to take home some unforgettable memories, you can do something local and capture the real flavor of the area. The following suggestions will give you a wide range of sights and experiences that won't take long, won't cost very much and will make your visit very special.

• **Walk across the Golden Gate Bridge** (➤ 42) from San Francisco to Marin County. Spend a few hours wandering around the town of Sausalito on the other side, then you can either walk or hop on a ferry back to San Francisco. Finish the day with a cable-car ride to view the city's marvelous architecture.

• **Spend a day hiking or backpacking** in one of the many national or state parks. The Joshua Tree National Monument is an especially good one (➤ 157).

• **Take a drive (or train)** along California's famous Route 1 for fantastic ocean views to the west and spectacular rolling hills or majestic mountain ranges to the east.

- **Visit a theme park**. Disneyland is the most well-known (➤ 40–41), but Balboa Park/San Diego Zoo is exciting too (➤ 36–37).

- **Go window-shopping** along Beverly Hills' exclusive Rodeo Drive (➤ 62) or El Paseo Drive in Palm Springs (➤ 62).

- **Take the one-day cruise** from San Pedro or Newport Beach to Catalina Island (➤ 38–39).

• **Take a drive through the Napa Valley** wine country, stopping at any of the vineyards for a tour and some wine-tasting (➤ 50–51). If you're the designated driver, most wineries sell bottles to take home.

• **Spend the day** at one of the many beaches. Surf, sun or rent a bicycle, boogieboard or rollerblades.

• **Experience the excitement** of professional sports in San Francisco, San Diego or Los Angeles or attend a horse race at one of the major tracks.

● **Tour one of Hollywood's** motion picture studios for an inside look at the making of screen magic. Universal Studios (➤ 142) is the most famous.

Planning

Before you go

WHEN TO GO

Los Angeles

JAN	FEB	MAR	APR	MAY	JUN	JUL	AUG	SEP	OCT	NOV	DEC
19°C	20°C	20°C	21°C	22°C	25°C	28°C	28°C	28°C	26°C	22°C	20°C
67°F	69°F	69°F	71°F	73°F	78°F	84°F	84°F	84°F	79°F	73°F	69°F

🌧️ High season 🌥️ Low season

Temperatures given above are the average daily maximum for each month in LA. California has a far more diverse climate than the image of sun and sand. Generally speaking, the south is warmer and the north cooler. The Bay Area and northern coast are renowned for their fog, especially in summer, making spring and autumn the best time, while the Sierra Nevada and Cascade mountains are pleasant during the summer but often snowbound over the winter. The San Joaquin and Sacramento valleys are baking hot during the summer, then moderate to cool the rest of the year. The deserts follow the usual pattern of hot, dry days and chilly nights. Most precipitation occurs from November through April.

WHAT YOU NEED

● Required
○ Suggested
▲ Not required

Some countries require a passport to remain valid for a minimum period (usually at least six months) beyond the date of entry – check before you travel.

	UK	Germany	USA	Netherlands	Spain
Passport (or National Identity Card where applicable)	●	●	▲	●	●
Visa (regulations can change – check before you travel)	▲	▲	▲	▲	▲
Onward or Return Ticket	●	●	▲	●	●
Health Inoculations	▲	▲	▲	▲	▲
Health Documentation (▶ 23, Health Insurance)	●	●	●	●	●
Travel Insurance	○	○	○	○	○
Driving License (national)	●	●	●	●	●
Car Insurance Certificate (if own vehicle)	○	○	○	○	○

WEBSITES

www.visitcalifornia.com
www.onlyinsanfrancisco.com
www.touringca.com
www.disneyland.com
www.lawa.org/lax

www.flysfo.com
www.nps.gov/redw/
www.nps.gov/yose/
www.latourist.com
www.shastacascade.com

TOURIST OFFICES AT HOME

In the UK

Visit USA Association
☎ 020/7495-4814
www.visitusa.org.uk

In the USA

California Division of Tourism
801 K Street, Suite 1600,
Sacramento, CA 95812
☎ 916/444-4429,
call-free 800/462-2543

HEALTH INSURANCE

There is no agreement for medical treatment between the US and other countries and all travelers MUST be covered by medical insurance (for an unlimited amount of medical costs is advisable). Treatment may be refused without evidence of insurance.

Medical insurance will cover you for dental treatment. In the event of any emergency, see your hotel concierge or consult the Yellow Pages for an emergency dentist.

TIME DIFFERENCES

California	USA (NY)	GMT	Germany	Netherlands	Spain
4AM	7AM	12 noon	1PM	1PM	1PM

California is on Pacific Standard Time (PST); eight hours behind Greenwich Mean Time (GMT-8), but from early April, when clocks are put forward one hour, to early November, Daylight Saving Time (GMT-7) operates. California is also three hours behind the east coast of the USA (Eastern Standard Time/EST).

PLANNING

NATIONAL HOLIDAYS

Jan 1 *New Year's Day*

Jan (3rd Mon) *Martin Luther King Jr's Birthday*

Feb 12 *Lincoln's Birthday*

Feb (3rd Mon) *President's Day*

Jul 4 *Independence Day*

Sep (1st Mon) *Labor Day*

Oct (2nd Mon) *Columbus Day*

Nov 11 *Veteran's Day*

Nov (4th Thu) *Thanksgiving Day*

Dec 25 *Christmas Day*

On these days shops, banks and businesses close.

WHAT'S ON WHEN

The following are just a few of California's myriad festivals and celebrations.

January *Tournament of Roses Parade*, Pasadena; www.tournamentofroses.com

Palm Springs International Film Festival; www.psfilmfest.org

February *Chinese New Year Celebration*, San Francisco; www.chineseparade.com

Napa Valley Mustard Celebration, Napa; www.mustardfestival.org

March *International Asian American Film Festival*, San Francisco; www.asianamericanmedia.org

Los Angeles Marathon; www.lamarathon.com

Mendocino Whale Festival; www.mendowhale.com

April *Toyota Grand Prix*, Long Beach; www.gplb.com

Cherry Blossom Festival, San Francisco; www.nccbf.org

Cinco De Mayo Celebration, state-wide

May *San Francisco International Film Fest;* www.sffs.org

Sacramento Jazz Jubilee; www.sacjazz.com

San Francisco Bay to Breakers, a race where people run in costume; www.baytobreakers.com

June *Scottish Highlands Games and Gathering of the Clans*, Modesto; www.standrewsmodesto.org

Amador County Wine Festival, Plymouth; www.amadorwine.com

July *Festival of Arts and Pageant of the Masters*, Laguna Beach; www.foapom.com
California Rodeo, Salinas; www.carodeo.com
Greek Festival, Santa Barbara; www.santabarbaragreekfestival.com
San Francisco Marathon; www.thesfmarathon.com
August *Mozart Festival*, San Luis Obispo; www.festivalmozaic.com
Sawdust Festival, Laguna Beach; www.sawdustartfestival.org
San Francisco Mime Troupe; www.sfmt.org
Summer Park Season
Old Spanish Days Fiesta, Santa Barbara; www.oldspanishdays-fiesta.org
Japanese Cultural Bazaar, Sacramento; www.buddhistchurch.com
California State Fair, Sacramento; www.bigfun.org
Children's Festival of the Arts, Hollywood; www.hollywoodartscouncil.org
September *Greek Food Festival*, Sacramento; www.sacrementogreekfestival.com
Oktoberfest, Huntington Beach; www.oldworld.ws
Danish Days, Solvang; www.solvangusa.com
Monterey Jazz Festival, Monterey; www.montereyjazzfestival.org
Bowlful of Blues Festival, Ojai; www.sbblues.org
California International Air Show, Salinas; www.salinasairshow.com
October *Jazz Festival*, San Francisco; www.sfjazz.org
Rose Show, Santa Barbara; www.sbrose.org
San Francisco Fleet week; www.fleetweek.us
November *West Coast Ragtime Festival*, Sacramento; www.westcoastragtime.com
Christmas Parade, Hollywood; www.thehollywoodchristmasparade.com
December *Newport Harbor Christmas Boat Parade*, Newport Beach; www.christmasboatparade.com
New Year's Eve Torchlight Parade, Big Bear Lake; www.eventsinbigbear.com

Getting there

BY AIR

Los Angeles Airport

15 miles (24km) to city center

45–60 minutes

35 minutes

30 minutes

San Francisco Airport

16 miles (26km) to city center

N/A

30–60 minutes

30 minutes

International direct flights operate into Los Angeles (LAX ☎ 310/646-5252) – one of the world's busiest airports – and San Francisco (SFO ☎ 650/821-8211). Oakland (OAK), San Diego (SAN) and San Jose (SJC) airports also receive international flights. For the Federal Aviation Authority's air safety hotline tel: 800/322-7873.

BY CAR

Interstates 10, 15, 40 and 80 are the main routes into the state from the east. Interstate 5 is the principal route that runs from north to south. Route 101 is the smaller, more scenic route to drive while traveling along the coast. In some places it turns into Route 1. All gas stations have detailed maps.

BY RAIL AND BUS

There are Amtrak railroad stations in or near most of the major cities in California that connect from Las Vegas and other large places in the southwest. Many travelers find this a sensible way to see the state. Of particular interest is the scenic route that follows the coastline – the Coast Starlight – from Seattle to Los Angeles or on to San Diego via Oakland, Salinas, San Luis Obispo, Santa Barbara and the Malibu coast. For the most up-to-date information visit www.amtrak.com or call 800/872-7245.

For information about the extensive network of Greyhound Lines long-distance buses tel: 800/231-2222; www.greyhound.com.

Getting around

PUBLIC TRANSPORTATION

Internal flights Flying is the quickest way of getting around California and is not all that expensive if you take advantage of deals offered by airlines. The international airports of San Francisco, Oakland, San Jose, Los Angeles and San Diego connect with a number of regional airports.

Trains Rail service is provided by America's National Railroad Corporation, Amtrak. Carriages are clean, comfortable and rarely crowded. A Far Western Region Rail Pass (available only outside the US) gives 45 days unlimited travel over the far Western states.

Long-distance buses Buses are by far the cheapest way of getting around. Greyhound Lines operates an inter-city service and also links many smaller towns within California. The Ameripass (only available outside the US) gives 4, 5, 7, 15, 30 or 60 days unlimited travel throughout the USA.

Ferries A ferry service links San Francisco with the Bay communities of Sausalito, Larkspur and Tiburon in scenic Marin County, and to Vallejo, Oakland and Alameda (departures from Pier 1, foot of Market Street). There is also a boat service from Long Beach and Newport Beach to Catalina Island.

Urban transportation Local communities and major cities are served by local bus services. In addition, San Francisco has cable-cars serving the downtown area and the BART train system covering the Bay areas. Los Angeles has its metrorail and San Diego has a trolley car service through the downtown area.

TAXIS

Cabs may be hailed on the street but few cruise outside tourist areas. If you are away from airports or major hotels it is best to phone for one (look under "cabs" in Yellow Pages). In most cities rates are high, except San Francisco because of its comparatively small size.

DRIVING

- Americans drive on the right.
- Seat belts must be worn in front seats at all times and in rear seats where fitted.
- Random breath-testing takes place. Never drive under the influence of alcohol.
- Fuel (gasoline or gas), leaded and unleaded, is sold in US gallons (3.8 liters). Most gas stations are self service. When removing the nozzle from the pump you must lift or turn the lever to activate it. Fuel is more expensive in remote areas and you may be charged more if paying by credit card.
- If you break down in a rented car, phone the emergency number on the dashboard. Summon help from emergency telephones located along freeways (every half mile) and remote highways (every 2 miles/3.2km), or sit tight and wait for the cruising highway patrol or state patrol to spot you (a raised bonnet should help).
- Speed limits are as follows:
  On rural interstate roads (motorways) 55–70mph (88–113kph)
  On many freeways (two-lane or more carriageways) 65mph (105kph)
  In residential and business districts and school zones 25mph (40kph)
  or as signposted

CAR RENTAL

If you are planning to rent a car, consider taking advantage of one of the fly/drive programs many airlines offer before you go. Otherwise most car rental companies have offices throughout the state. Charges depend on the size of car, locale and time of year. Most companies require a credit card as a deposit.

None of the major companies will rent to anyone under the age of 25. It may be possible to find a local company that will do so, but be prepared to pay a loaded insurance premium.

It is advisable to find out whether your own insurance would cover damage to a rented car, and what the details are of Collision Damage Waiver (CDW).

FARES AND CONCESSIONS

Students Upon production of ID proving student status, there are discounts available on travel, theater and museum tickets, plus at some nightspots. It is always worth asking at the outset.

Senior citizens For anyone over the age of 62 there is a tremendous variety of discounts on offer (upon proof of age). Both Amtrak (train) and Greyhound (bus), as well as many US airlines, offer (smallish) percentage reductions on fares. Museums, art galleries, attractions, cinemas, and even hotels offer small discounts, and as the definition of senior can drop to as low as 55, it is always worth enquiring.

Being there

TOURIST OFFICES

Anaheim/Orange County Visitor &
Convention Bureau, 800 West
Katella Avenue, Anaheim, CA 92802
☎ 714/765-8888;
www.anaheimoc.org

California Deserts Tourism
Association, 37–115 Palm View
Road, Rancho Mirage, CA 92270
☎ 760/328-9256;
www.californiadeserts.org

Los Angeles Convention & Visitors
Bureau, 685 Figueroa Street,
Los Angeles, CA 90017
☎ 213/689-8822;
www.discoverlosangeles.com

Sacramento Convention & Visitors
Bureau, 1608 I Street, Sacramento,
CA 95814
☎ 916/264-7777;
www.sacramento365.com

San Diego Convention & Visitors
Bureau, 401 B Street, Suite 1400,
San Diego, CA 92101
☎ 619/236-1212;
www.sandiego.org

San Francisco Convention & Visitors
Bureau, 201 Third Street, Suite 900,
San Francisco, CA 94103
☎ 415/974-6900; www.sfcvb.org

MONEY

The American monetary unit is the dollar ($), which is divided into 100
cents. There are coins of 1 cent (penny), 5 cents (nickel), 10 cents
(dime), 25 cents (quarter), 50 cents (half dollar) and 1 dollar. Bills (notes)
are available in denominations of 1, 2 (rarely seen), 5, 10, 20, 50 and
100 dollars.

POSTAL AND INTERNET SERVICES

Post offices are plentiful in cities. Stamps are also sold from stamp
machines in hotels and shops but have a 25 percent mark up. Main post
offices in larger cities normally open 8–6 (noon Sat), closed Sun;
☎ 213/483-3745 (Los Angeles), ☎ 415/487-8981 (San Francisco). Smaller
branches open Mon–Fri 9–5:30, Sat 9–12:30.

Most accommodations offer WiFi access, usually free, as do many
cafés. Public libraries also have computers with free internet access.

TIPS/GRATUITIES

Yes ✓   No ✗

Restaurants	✓	15–20%
Cafeterias/fast-food outlets	✗	
Bars	✓	15–20%
Cabs	✓	15–20%
Porters	✓	$1 per bag
Chambermaids	✓	$1 per day
Toilet attendants	✗	

TELEPHONES

Telephones are located in hotel and motel lobbies, drugstores, restaurants, garages and in roadside kiosks. Exact change in 5, 10 and 25 cent pieces is required to place a call. For internal calls dial 1 before the number when the area code is different from the one on the phone you are using. For the operator dial 0, for directory assistance dial 411.

International Dialling Codes

From the USA to:
UK: 011 44
Germany: 011 49
Netherlands: 011 31
Spain: 011 34

Emergency telephone numbers

Police 911
Fire 911
Ambulance 911

EMBASSIES AND CONSULATES

UK ☎ 310/481-0031 (LA)
Germany ☎ 323/930-2703 (LA),
☎ 415/775-1061 (SF)

Netherlands ☎ 310/268-1598 (LA)
Spain ☎ 323/938-0158 (LA),
☎ 415/922-2995 (SF)

HEALTH ADVICE

Sun advice California enjoys a lot of sunshine with more than 250 clear days a year at least in the south. Along the coast mornings can be hazily overcast and sea breezes (especially in the north) can make it feel cooler than it is. Protect the skin at all times.

Drugs Quick-remedy medicines such as aspirin are readily available at any pharmacy (drugstore). For tablets containing acetaminophen look for paracetamol. Also, many pain-killing pills available "over the counter" at home may need a prescription in the US.

Safe water It is quite safe to drink tap water. In hotels and restaurants water, generally ice cold, is provided free with meals. Bottled water is also widely available but is not as popular as in Europe.

PERSONAL SAFETY

California is certainly not crime free and drugs are a problem, but exercise due caution, especially in downtown areas, and you should be safe. Away from these areas crime is quite low key. Some precautions:

● If confronted by a mugger, hand over your money.
● If driving do not stop the car in any unlit or deserted urban area.
● Police assistance: ☎ 911 from any call box

ELECTRICITY

The power supply is 110–115 volts. Round 3-hole sockets taking plugs with 2 flat pins in a parallel position, with an upper, round, earth pin for earthed appliances. European visitors should bring a voltage transformer as well as an adaptor.

OPENING HOURS

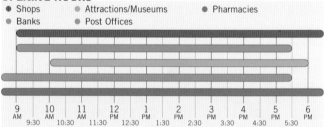

In addition to the times shown above, many shops, particularly department stores within shopping malls, are open evenings and during afternoons on Sunday. Some supermarkets and grocery shops open 24 hours. Banks open until 5:30pm Friday and some major banks open on Saturday. Banks in some major towns and tourist areas may have longer hours. Some pharmacies open from 7am to 9pm or even midnight, while some open 24 hours. Opening times of attractions and museums vary (see individual entries in the What to See section). Some post offices open Saturday 8am–1pm.

LANGUAGE

English is the official language of the USA. Californians, however, are a fascinating mix of cultures, most notably of Spanish or Mexican extraction. In fact, Spanish is heard throughout California. The five largest cities in California: Los Angeles, San Diego, San Francisco, San Jose and Sacramento bear Spanish names. You are unlikely to encounter any problems communicating in English but it can still be useful to have some basic Mexican–Spanish. Some helpful words and phrases are:

Hello! Good morning	*Hola! Buenos días!*	Please/thank you	*Por favor/gracias*
Good afternoon	*Buenas tardes!*	It's a pleasure	*De nada*
Good night	*Buenas noches!*	I don't speak Spanish	*No hablo español*
Goodbye/see you	*Adiós/hasta luego*	Do you speak English?	*¿Habla inglés?*
Yes/no	*Sí/no*		
Do you have a single/double room?	*¿Tiene una habitación sencilla/doble?*	For two nights	*Para dos noches*
		With fan/air-conditioning	*Con ventilador/aire acondicionado*
With a balcony/sea view	*Con balcon/vista al mar*	Is there a swimming-pool	*¿Hay una alberca?*
How much does it cost?	*¿Cuánto cuesta?/ Cuánta se cobre?*	Do you take credit cards?	*¿Accepta tarjetas de crédito?*
Very expensive/cheap/too much	*Muy caro/barato/ demasiado*	Where is the nearest bank?	*Dónde esta el banco mas cerca?*
Can I have the menu/bill, please?	*El menu/la cuenta por favor*	A cup of black coffee with milk	*Un café americano/ con leche*
We'll have two beers please	*Dos cervezas por favor*	Fruit juice	*Un jugo de fruta*
Fizzy mineral water	*Un agua mineral*	A bottle of red/white wine	*Una botella de vino tinto/blanco*
Where is the bus station?	*¿Dónde esta el central camionera?*	How far is the nearest petrol station?	*¿A qué distancia esta la gasolinera mas cerca?*
Straight on/to the left/to the right	*Todo derecho/a la izquierda/a la derecha*	How long is the journey?	*¿Cuánto tiempo dura el viaje?*

Best places to see

Balboa Park

This immense expanse of parks and museums includes the world-renowned San Diego Zoo.

A 100-tone chime serenades from the 200ft (61m) California Tower, creating an exquisite backdrop for the historical buildings, museums and gardens of this 1,200-acre (486ha) park. Start your visit from the main thoroughfare, El Prado (The Promenade). Here you'll find original exhibit halls from the 1915 Panama–California International Exposition, most notably the Casa del Prado. The **Timken Museum of Art**, a few blocks south, has interesting Russian icons among its exhibits.

At the park's center are several small museums: **San Diego History Center**, **Museum of Photographic Arts**, **Model Railroad Museum** and **Hall of Champions** (sports). The nearby Reuben H. Fleet Space Theater and Science Center provides hands-on exhibits for youngsters. The **Natural History Museum** features exhibits of southwest desert and marine life, and at the end of the plaza are The Museum of Man (➤ 169) and the **San Diego Museum of Art**.

Be sure to visit any of the three stages of the Globe Theatre to see contemporary or Shakespearean plays, or enjoy a summer musical at The Starlight Bowl.

Simply stated, the **San Diego Zoo** is among the finest zoos in the world. The 100 acres (40ha) simulate the natural habitats of the 800 species living here, and allows expansive roaming of its 4,000 animals, which include the only pair of pandas in the US. The Children's Zoo offers

close-up views. There are guided bus tours, as well as an aerial tramway that rises 170ft (52m) over the zoo's grottoes and mesas, providing a fine overview of the park.

➕ 11Z ✉ 1 mile (1.61km) north of downtown San Diego
☎ 619/239-0512 🕓 Daily 9–4:30 (4 in winter)
✋ Moderate 🚌 7, 7A or 7B from downtown ❓ Visitor Center sells multi-day passports to the park; free in-park tram

Timken Museum of Art
☎ 619/239-5548; www.timkenmuseum.org 🕓 Tue–Sat 10–4:30, Sun 1:30–4:30 ✋ Free

San Diego History Center
☎ 619/232-6203; www.sandiegohistory.org 🕓 Tue–Sun 10–5 ✋ Inexpensive

Museum of Photographic Arts
☎ 619/238-7559; www.mopa.org 🕓 Tue–Sun 10–5 ✋ Inexpensive

Model Railroad Museum
☎ 619/696-0119; www.sdmodelrailroadm.com 🕓 Tue–Fri 11–4, Sat–Sun 11–5 ✋ Inexpensive

Hall of Champions
☎ 619/234-2544; www.sdhoc.com 🕓 Daily 10–4:30 ✋ Inexpensive

Natural History Museum
☎ 619/282-3821; www.sdnhm.org 🕓 Daily 10–5 ✋ Moderate

San Diego Museum of Art
☎ 619/232-7931; www.sdmart.org 🕓 Tue–Sat 10–5 (Thu until 9 in summer), Sun noon–5 ✋ Moderate

San Diego Zoo
☎ 619/234-3153; www.sandiegozoo.com 🕓 Daily mid-Jun to early Sep 9–8; early Sep to mid-June 9–4 ✋ Expensive

2 Catalina Island

Known as "The Island of Romance," Catalina Island is a perfect blend of relaxed resort, pristine shoreline and untouched wilderness.

Discovered in 1542 by Juan Rodriguez Cabrillo, Santa Catalina (commonly called Catalina Island) is now officially part of Los Angeles County but lies roughly 26 miles (42km) from the mainland. One of

the eight California Channel Islands, it is 21 miles (34km) long and 8 miles (13km) wide. No cars are allowed on the island, so use the public transportation or rent the electric golf carts and bicycles available.

In 1811, the indigenous Gabrileño Indians were forced to resettle on the mainland, leaving the island that later became the private property of the Wrigley family, the chewing gum heirs. Today, 86 percent of the island is owned by the non-profit Santa Catalina Island Conservancy, established in 1972 to preserve the island's natural beauty. The island provides a welcome retreat from mainland crowds, with its silent beaches, watersports, picturesque pier and deep-sea fishing.

The 1929 Avalon Casino is the most famous building on the island, best known for its art deco ballroom, which in its heyday was host to many of the world's most famous orchestras and big bands. The Catalina Island Museum, on the first floor of the Casino, exhibits the island's history. The Wrigley Mansion, with its botanical gardens, and the Avalon Pier, in the middle of Avalon Bay, provide fine views of the interior hills and the breathtaking shoreline

✚ 9Y 🏛 Travel moderate; exhibits inexpensive
🍴 Restaurants ($$–$$$) 🚢 Catalina Express 310/579-7971 or 800/481-3470; 1 hour each way; hourly from San Pedro or Long Beach.Catalina Flyer 800/830-7744; 75 mins each way; departs from Balboa Pavilion 9, returns 4:30
❌ Helicopter Service from Island Express 800/228-2566; 15 mins each way
ℹ Green Pier; tel: 310/510-1520; www.catalina.com; daily 8–5

3 Disneyland® Resort

www.disneyland.com

Disneyland Resort sets the standard for theme parks. This "happiest place on earth" attracts around 12 million visitors each year.

Children and adults alike are enchanted by the illusion and entertainment of "magic kingdom," opened in 1955. The 80-acre (32ha) park is divided into eight sections, offering such diverse attractions as fantasy rides, musical performances, parades, restaurants and shops.

Pastel-colored walkways lead from the central plaza at the end of Main Street, U.S.A. into the themed areas, each with their own attractions. Mickey's Toontown brings out the kid in everyone; Adventureland offers a jungle cruise and the Enchanted Tiki Room. New Orleans Square has a boat ride through the Pirates of the Caribbean attraction and the Haunted Mansion. For the more courageous, the Indiana Jones Adventure takes you on a

journey to the Temple of the Forbidden Eye.

In Frontierland, you can careen down Big Thunder Mountain Railroad on a runaway train or raft across to Tom Sawyer Island. Critter Country is the home of the Splash Mountain flume ride. Fantasyland begins when you cross the moat to Sleeping Beauty Castle, while Tomorrowland explores the future with thrilling attractions like Space Mountain and Star Tours. Disney characters roam the streets and willingly pose for photographs.

Disneyland Resort is now even bigger and better with the addition of the Disney California Adventure Park.

➕ 10X, ✉ 1313 Harbor Boulevard, Anaheim ☎ 714/781-4565 🕓 Peak season Mon–Fri 9am–midnight (until 1am Sat; low season Mon–Fri 10–6 (until 9pm weekends, public hols). Hours can vary, check first 💰 Expensive ❓ Hours and prices subject to change; on busy days park at the Disneyland Hotel and ride the monorail to the park

4 Golden Gate Bridge and National Recreation Area

The Golden Gate Bridge is quite easily the most beautiful and easily recognized bridge in the world.

The rust-colored symbol of the West Coast stands as a beacon at the entrance of San Francisco Bay. Built in 1937 it is impressive from any angle. Often cloaked in fog, the suspension bridge is graceful and delicate in design even though its overall length is 8,981ft (2,737m), and the stolid towers reach 746ft (227m) high. Connecting San Francisco to Marin County and northern California, the bridge withstands winds of up to 100mph (161kph) and swings as much as 27ft (8m). Enjoy the drive over, or walk across for a truly spectacular perspective.

The Golden Gate National Recreation Area is the largest conglomeration of urban parks in the US, and covers 74,000 acres (29,959ha) from San Mateo County to Tomales Bay. The giant recreation area offers many attractions, including Fort Mason on San Francisco's waterfront. A former military embarkation point for soldiers during World War II, today the fort is the site of museums, theaters, galleries, restaurants and the last unaltered, operational liberty ship, the SS *Jeremiah O'Brien*.

The Golden Gate Promenade is a scenic bayshore hike stretching 3.5 miles (5.5km) from Hyde Street Pier to Fort Point and beyond, across the Golden Gate Bridge. Among other sights in this impressive area are The Presidio, Baker Beach, Cliff House, Ocean Beach and Fort Funston, most of which are accessible by San Francisco's MUNI system.

✚ 3H

Golden Gate Bridge ☎ MUNI 28; 415/554-6999 (hotline);
www.goldengatebridge.org ✋ Free northbound;
southbound toll inexpensive

Recreation Area

✉ GGNRA, Building 201, Fort Mason, San Francisco
☎ 415/561-4700 (information line); www.nps.gov/goga
🕐 Mon–Fri 9:30–4:30 ✋ Moderate 🍴 Cafés, stands ($)

5 Hearst Castle

www.hearstcastle.com

William Randolph Hearst's tribute to excess and grandiosity crowns a hillside above the village of San Simeon.

The history of this fabulous castle dates back to 1865, when George Hearst purchased 40,000 acres

rst Castle© CA State Parks

(16,194ha) of Mexican land adjacent to San Simeon Bay. His son, newspaper magnate William Randolph Hearst, began the castle when he took possession of the land in 1919, which now numbers 250,000 acres

(101,215ha). Steamers and chain-driven trucks were used to transport materials to the remote spot, but the palatial residence was not completed until 1947.

Casa Grande, as the mammoth mansion is called, boasts more than 100 rooms filled with priceless objects of art and antiques. It was donated to the California Park Service in 1957.

Among the mansion's exquisite attributes are Gothic fireplaces, Flemish tapestries, Renaissance paintings and ceilings ranging in style from 16th-century Spanish to 18th-century Italian. In its prime, the doge's suite was reserved for the most important guests: presidents, visiting heads of state such as Winston Churchill and Hollywood luminaries. Marble colonnades and statuary flanking the indoor and outdoor pools replicate figures of antiquity.

There are also five greenhouses with over 700,000 annuals providing year-round color, tennis courts and a movie theater (in which Walt Disney hosted the first screening of *Snow White* in 1938). Other facilities include two libraries, riding stables and the world's largest private zoo.

✚ 5L ✉ 750 Hearst Castle Road, San Simeon ☎ 805/927-2020 or 800/444-4445
🕐 Daily 8:20–3:20 (Dec start times may vary). Five different tours offered daily
✋ Expensive ❓ 214 miles (345km) southeast of San Francisco; 242 miles (390km) northwest of Los Angeles; parking just off Hwy 1 with shuttles buses to the castle. Four tours, priced separately. Tour 1 is recommended for first-time visitors. Reservations suggested

Hollywood

A one-time cow town, Hollywood is now the movie-making capital of the world and trend-setting center of glamour, glitter and excess.

Hollywood Boulevard is a relatively short street, but is one of the best known of all Los Angeles thoroughfares. Its wealth of art deco architecture has elevated it to the status of national historic district. From the 1920s to the 1950s, Hollywood boasted some of the country's largest movie palaces and exclusive department stores. As the movie industry expanded outward, Hollywood lost its luster, but the faded star is now staging a comeback.

The Hollywood Roosevelt Hotel, site of the first Academy Awards, has been renovated and displays historical film memorabilia throughout. An ambitious three-block redevelopment project around Sid Grauman's

1927 Chinese Theatre (now Mann's Chinese Theatre; ➤ 140–141) offers shops, restaurants, movie theaters and the Hollywood Studio Museum.

Hollywood abounds with guided bus tours of every sort. Walking tours of its bronze-starred Walk of Fame are extremely popular. Begun in 1960 with only eight stars, there are now close to 3,000 celebrity handprints. The 1920s Hollywood sign can best be viewed by venturing up Beachwood Canyon on the eastern edge of Hollywood or from Griffith Observatory, high atop Mount Hollywood.

Paramount Studio provides a peek into the world of film-making. Free tickets to several popular TV shows are readily available outside Mann's Theatre or through the major network studios.

Hawkers along Sunset and Hollywood boulevards offer surprisingly accurate maps to celebrity homes at a low price; you can drive yourself or take a bus tour but they are far too spread out to consider walking.

➕ 9W ❓ LA TOURS tel: 323/937-3661; Hollywood Chamber of Commerce tel: 323/469-8311
ℹ️ 333 South Hope Street; tel: 213/624-7300

7 Monterey Peninsula

"This is the California men dreamed of years ago. The face of the earth as the Creator intended it to look." Henry Miller

For more than 300 years the Monterey Peninsula has enchanted everyone who has seen it. Formed by the Monterey and Carmel bays, the peninsula juts into the Pacific Ocean 120 miles (194km) south of San Francisco. Pristine beaches, craggy rock formations and wind- and wave-warped cypresses make the area among the most popular scenic spots in the world.

Nowhere in California is the state's Latin heritage more prevalent than in Monterey, where its exquisitely restored adobe buildings give testimony to the Spanish and Mexican periods of California history.

From art galleries in Carmel (➤ 122) to the grand estates in the dense woods of the Del Monte

Forest, the scenic 17-Mile Drive through the forest between Pacific Grove and Carmel is almost incomparable in beauty.

The legacy of famed California author John Steinbeck can be traced at The National Steinbeck Center in Salinas (➤ 124). You can also visit his preserved cottage in nearby Pacific Grove.

Carmel-by-the-Sea is an enchanting seaside village. Much of its architecture is reminiscent of rural European and early California styles.

Monterey's touristy Fisherman's Wharf has a magnificent promenade of fish markets, seafood restaurants, shops and theaters. For a different perspective, a sail can be arranged aboard the restored tall ship *Californian*.

Established at the turn of the 20th century by a group of writers and artists, Carmel was originally a planned resort. As its popularity soared, it took on the reputation of something completely different: an exclusive bohemian retreat. Resisting efforts for modernization, Carmel has preserved its idyllic setting. At Point Lobos State Reserve, 2 miles (3.5km) south of Carmel, harbor seals, gray whales and California sea lions frolic among a variety of sea birds and pelicans, a sight seen nowhere else in the world.

✚ 4K ✉ 122 miles (197km) southeast of San Francisco; 334 miles (539km) northwest of LA ☎ State Historical Park 831/649-7118; Carmel Business Association 831/624-2522; Steinbeck Country Tours 831/659-0333 🚌 Monterey–Salinas Transit
ℹ tel: 877/666-8373; www.seemonterey.com

8 Napa Valley

Only 30 miles (48km) long and 3 miles (5km) across at its widest, this little valley boasts some 220 wineries.

Leader of the American wine industry, the Napa Valley boasts such well-known names as Robert Mondavi, Domaine Chandon, Beringer and Sterling. Although the greatest concentration of wineries is along State Route 29, north from Napa to Calistoga, knowledgeable travelers use the Silverado Trail, a scenic, vineyard-lined parallel road along the eastern edge of the valley.

The city of Napa is the largest settlement, although the smaller valley towns are more charming. In Calistoga there are spas and geysers, one of which shoots 60ft (18m) into the air every 40 minutes. St. Helena claims many of the region's best dining and lodging choices, as well as a wine library and the Silverado Museum. An ancient volcanic eruption from Washington's Mount St. Helens around 3 million years ago caused the giant redwoods of California to become instantly petrified. You'll find the Petrified Forest between Calistoga and Santa Rosa.

Outside of these towns lie more wineries, markets, inns, quiet picnic areas and historic parklands. Most visitors to the area tour the vineyards, which offer a look at the wine-making process and feature wine-tastings, but there are also five different walking tours of the incredible architectural highlights of the valley (maps available at the visitor information center). If possible, avoid the crowded summer weekends. Most vintners now charge a small fee for the tastings and a few require reservations.

🚻 4G 🍴 Many restaurants in the towns ($$–$$$)
❓ Napa Valley Wine Train: tel: 800/427-4124; www.winetrain.com; moderate. Tours: hours vary and some require reservations; moderate
🏠 1310 Napa Town Center, Napa; tel: 07/226-7459 or 707/253-2111; www.napavalley.com

9 Redwood National Park

www.nps.gov/redw/

A vast forest of giant redwoods grows naturally nowhere else in the country except in this coastal region.

Before California's famous gold rush, and the resulting surge of new population, the world's tallest trees blanketed an area 30 miles (48km) wide and 450 miles (726km) long. The majority of today's redwood "stands" are along US 101, from Leggett north to Crescent City. It is about a five-hour drive from San Francisco to the southern edge of the Redwood Forest, via the scenic coastal highway.

A small segment of old growth redwoods and outstanding coastal scenery have been protected in the 106,000-acre (42,915ha) Redwood National Park. Eight miles (13km) of shoreline roads and more than 150 miles (242km) of trails afford close-up encounters with these trees and the abundant plant and animal life they nurture.

The three main state parks within the Park's boundaries are Prairie Creek, Del Norte Coast and Jedediah Smith. Campers favor Prairie Creek

because of its herds of native Roosevelt elk and expansive beach (Gold Bluffs Beach). Lady Bird Johnson Cove is especially beautiful. Don't miss the Libby Tree, the tallest known tree, which towers to over 368ft (112m).

A drive through Del Norte Coast park allows you to enjoy spectacular ocean views and the inland forest simultaneously. The giant redwoods grow closest to the shoreline at the Damnation Creek Trail. In the spring, this area is the best place to view the abundant growth of rhododendrons and azaleas.

At the north end of the park, the Jedediah Smith terrain gives you an elevated perspective.

➕ 2B ✉ National Park Headquarters, 1111 Second Street, Crescent City ☎ 707/464-6101 (Redwood National Park Information Center) ✋ Free–moderate 🍴 Restaurants ($); picnic facilities

10 Yosemite National Park

www.nps.gov/yose/

By any standards, Yosemite is the most spectacular national park in the country. To call it awe-inspiring would be an understatement.

Nearly 70 percent of the annual visitors to Yosemite National Park arrive in the summer and stay within the compact but awesome Yosemite Valley. The main section of the park, just 7sq miles (18sq km) in area, boasts monumental granite walls and high-diving waterfalls, but there remains almost 1,200sq miles (3,076sq km) of splendor to explore. Beyond are such natural wonders as giant sequoias, alpine meadows, lakes and trout-filled streams, Glacier Point and majestic 13,000ft (3,963m) Sierra Nevada peaks. Giant sequoias are located in the Mariposa

Grove, near the park's south entrance, about 30 miles (48km) from Yosemite Valley. In this great forest, over 200 trees measure more than 10ft (3m) in diameter.

Some of the park's finest scenery is in the wild back country along the Tioga Road. There are rustic lodges and campgrounds (permit camping). In the main valley, 3,500ft (1,067m) El Capitan attracts climbers from around the world.

Off-season visits are also spectacular. In fall, leaves turn from green to crimson and gold and

nights are cool and pleasant. Spring offers stunning waterfalls that create rainbows across the valley floor. For the ambitious, there's the 200-mile (322km) John Muir Trail that follows the naturalist's path through the wilderness. For many, the winter provides solitude and restores the raw grandeur of the park. The ski season at Badger Pass lasts from the end of November until mid-April.

🕂 8Q 🚫 Park access unrestricted 🖐 Moderate
🍴 Restaurants ($)
ℹ Yosemite Valley Visitors Center, Yosemite Village; tel: 209/372-0200; Jun–Sep 9–7; Oct–9–5

Best things to do

Good places to have lunch

♦♦ Diego's ($)

If touring the Gold Country, this is a great place to stop for a spicy Mexican empanada, sandwich, tasty fish taco or choice of salads.
✉ 217 Colfax Avenue, Grass Valley ☎ 530/477-1460; www.diegosrestaurant.com

♦♦ Dottie's True Blue Café ($)

The frequent queues outside this legendary downtown diner stand as a testament to the quality of the generous all-day breakfasts and lunch specials.
✉ 525 Jones Street, San Francisco ☎ 415/885-2767

☆☆ Fat City Bar & Café ($$)

Located in Old Sacramento, the 100-year-old bar and stained glass windows provide a fine backdrop to the tasty food.

✉ 1001 Front Street, Sacramento ☎ 916/446-6768

☆☆ Locanda Veneta ($)

Imaginative Italian cuisine, where you can try the set "Power Lunch" or "Perfect Lunch", on the west side of downtown.

✉ 8638 West 3rd Street, Los Angeles ☎ 310/274-1893;
www.locandaveneta.net

☆☆ Miramar Beach Restaurant ($$)

With a lovely setting on the ocean side of the Peninsula, this place serves up fine seafood and pasta.

✉ 131 Mirada Road, Half Moon Bay ☎ 650/726-9053;
www.miramarbeachrestaurant.com

☆☆ Opal Restaurant & Bar ($)

A snazzy restaurant that does surprisingly good-value lunch specials, sandwiches, pizzas and the odd Asian dish.

✉ 1325 State Street, Santa Barbara ☎ 805/966-9676;
www.opalrestaurantandbar.com

☆☆ Samoa Cookhouse ($)

If you're in the Eureka area, don't miss the gut-busting set meals at this old–time spot, once frequented by ravernous loggers. You'll never leave hungry.

✉ 908 Vance Avenue, Samoa ☎ 707/442-1659; www.samoacookhouse.net

☆☆☆ Tarpy's Roadhouse ($$)

Get a full-blown portion of meatloaf, ribs or steak, or settle for a filling sandwich or lighter salad.

✉ 2999 Monterey–Salinas Highway, Monterey ☎ 831/647-1444;
www.tarpys.com

Unusual annual events

February
National Date Festival Riverside County Fair, Indio: Since 1947, people have come from far and wide for ten days of fun that include ostrich and camel races.
☎ 760/863-8247; www.datefest.org

March
Snowfest, Tahoe City: The West's largest snow festival includes activities at the area's famous ski centers like Squaw Valley and Northstar, as well as events in town.
☎ 530/546-5253; www.tahoesnowfestival.com

Mendocino/Fort Bragg Whale Festival: This gathering affords the chance to watch the grey whale migration, taste wine and sample delights like seafood chowder.
☎ 707/961-6300; www.mendowhale.com

May

Calaveras County Fair & Jumping Frog Jubilee, Angel's Camp:
A huge purpose–built complex hosts the fair with a heritage dating
back to 1800's. The centerpiece is the jumping amphibians
immortalized by Mark Twain.
☎ 209/736-2561; www.frogtown.org

Great Monterey Squid Festival, Monterey: Good eating is the main
feature of this event, either in the eight-legged shape of the
cephalopods or other marine fare.
☎ 831/649-6547; www.monterey.com

July

Gilroy Garlic Festival, Gilroy: You can guarantee there won't be any
vampires in attendance at this festival, which features dishes
suffused with garlic.
☎ 408/842-1625; www.gilroygarlicfestival.com

October

Grand National Rodeo, Horse and Stock Show, Daly City (world-
class): Lots of Wild West fun from rodeo to other horsey events,
right on the edge of cultured San Francisco.
☎ 415/404-4100; www.nationalrodeo.com

Art & Pumpkin Festival, Half Moon Bay: For over 40 years, all
things pumpkin have been celebrated here, from weighing the
biggest to carving them imaginatively.
☎ 650/728-8380; www.miramarevents.com/pumpkinfest

November

Doo Dah Parade, Pasadena: This spoof of Pasadena's famous
Rose Parade includes lots of music, drinking and general
merriment.
☎ 626/440-7379; www.pasadenadoodahparade.info

Best shopping areas

LOS ANGELES
Melrose Avenue
Three-mile (5km) strip of shops, from Aardvark's used clothing to vintage stores and upscale boutiques.
➕ W9 ✉ Between Highland and Doheny, Hollywood

Rodeo Drive
Renowned as being the most exclusive and expensive shopping area on the West Coast. Top designer clothes and accessories.
➕ W9 ✉ Between Santa Monica and Wilshire boulevards, Beverly Hills; www.rodeodrive-bh.com

MONTEREY
Cannery Row
Unique shops and restaurants line this nautical area, made famous by John Steinbeck's novel *Cannery Row*.
➕ K4 ✉ Fisherman's Wharf; www.canneryrow.com

ORANGE COUNTY
South Coast Plaza
This is Orange County's largest and most exclusive mall, with three huge sections connected by a free tram. All major department stores are within this complex, along with a wide variety of specialty stores.
➕ X10; www.southcoastplaza.com

PALM SPRINGS
El Paseo
Exclusive shops that rival Beverly Hills' Rodeo Drive. Art galleries.
➕ X11 ✉ Visitors Center, 2901 N Palm Canyon Drive
☎ 760/778-8418; www.palmsprings.com/elpaseo

SAN DIEGO
Fashion Valley Mall
This and Mission Valley are the city's two main shopping centers. Six department stores.

➕ Z11 ✉ 352 Fashion Valley Road

Gaslamp Quarter
A must for the arts and crafts crowd. The Quarter takes in 38 acres (15ha) in the National Historic District.

➕ Z11 ✉ Fifth Avenue from Broadway to the waterfront; www.gaslamp.org

Old Town
Small gift boutiques and cafés among flower gardens, fountains and courtyards in the style of a Mexican marketplace. One of the best antiques shopping areas in Southern California with bargain prices for valuable items.

➕ Z11 ✉ Mason Street and San Diego Avenue

SAN FRANCISCO
Chinatown
Asian specialty shops, fresh produce, and incredible architecture (➤ 84–85).

➕ 4c ✉ Bordered by Broadway, Bush, Kearny and Powell streets

Fisherman's Wharf
Street performers entertain as you explore the 100 shops and restaurants clustered around the piers (➤ 83).

➕ 2a ✉ Between The Embarcadero and Columbus Avenue; www.fishermanswharf.com

Movie locations

Alcatraz Island, San Francisco – *The Birdman of Alcatraz* (1962); *Escape From Alcatraz* (1979); *The Rock* (1996)

Carney's, 12601 Ventura Boulevard, Studio City – *Crash* (2005)

D Street, Petaluma – *American Graffiti* (1973)

Golden Gate Bridge, San Francisco – *A View to A Kill* (1985); *The Bridge* (2006)

Muir Woods, Marin County – *Vertigo* (1958)

Regent Beverly Wiltshire Hotel, Wiltshire Boulevard, Los Angeles
– *Beverly Hills Cop* (1984); *Pretty Woman* (1990)

Union Station, Figueroa Street, downtown Los Angeles – *The Way We Were* (1973); *Blade Runner* (1982); *Bugsy* (1991)

Santa Barbara Wine Country – *Sideways* (2004)

Van Nuys Airport, 16461 Sherman Way, Van Nuys, San Fernando Valley – *Casablanca* (1942)

Venice Beach, Los Angeles – *The Doors* (1991)

Best beaches

East Beach The most centrally located of Santa Barbara's beaches, with lots of activities. ✚ W8

La Jolla Small, private beaches set in between cliffs. ✚ Y11

Laguna Beach Quaint, artistic community. Spacious beaches and coves, ideal for watching sea lions. ✚ X10

Newport–Huntington beaches Orange County's largest and most popular beach areas. Lots of boating opportunities. Huntington is also known for its international surfing and volleyball tournaments. ✚ X10

Ocean Beach Less crowded San Diego beach with great shops and restaurants. ✚ Z11

Pacific Beach Known to the locals as "PB." A large area with shopping and restaurants; also close to San Diego's attractions. ✚ Z11

Santa Cruz Beach California's only beach area with an amusement park on its boardwalk. Roller-coasters, bumper cars, haunted castles, Ferris wheel. ✚ J4

Santa Monica Beach Large accessible beach for those visiting LA and Hollywood. Long cycle path connects to Venice Beach to the south. ✚ W9

Stinson Beach North of San Francisco, with state park access and hiking trails. Cold in winter; perfect in summer. ✚ H3

Zuma Beach At the north end of Malibu. Excellent for surfing, volleyball and whale-watching during winter. ✚ W9

Places to take the children

California's Great America
The Bay area's place for roller coasters and other daredevil rides. Kidzville is an interactive parent/child area. Delerium and Invertigo rides are the most popular. Also features stage shows, musicals, puppet shows and wildlife shows.

✉ Great American Parkway, Santa Clara, south of San Francisco ☎ 408/988-1776; www.cagreatamerica.com 🕓 Sat–Sun 10–7; weekdays summer only ✋ Expensive

Charles Paddock Zoo and Atascadero Lake Park
Small zoo with jaguars from Brazil, Bengal tigers, pink flamingos and lots of chimps. Next to the zoo is a lake with picnic facilities.

✉ State Route 41, south of Paso Robles ☎ 805/461-5080; www.charlespaddockzoo.org 🕓 Zoo: daily 10–4 (until 5 in summer). Lake Park: daily until dusk ✋ Inexpensive

Disneyland Park
See pages 40–41.

Kidseum
Kids won't even realize they're being educated about world cultures as they take part in the story-telling, puppet shows and other exhibits at this interactive museum.

✉ 1802 Main Street, Santa Ana ☎ 714/480-1520 (Bowers Museum and College of Art); www.bowers.org/kidseum 🕓 Fri 10–4, Sat, Sun 11–4, Tue–Thu by appointment ✋ Inexpensive

Lake Nacimiento Resort
Great outdoor activities, including fishing and diving. Features a full-service marina and dock where you can rent anything from paddle boats to jet-skis to pontoon boats. Lodge, campgrounds and RV facilities.

✉ County Road G–14 out of Paso Robles ☎ 800/323-3839; www.nacimientoresort.com 🕓 Daily to dusk ✋ Prices vary

Legoland California

This Danish import opened in 1999, and the entire park is built out of lego pieces. Over 50 rides, exhibits and shows to choose from. Usually very packed.

✉ 1 Lego Drive, Carlsbad ☎ 760/918-5346; www.legoland.com 🕒 Call for hours 🖐 Expensive

Raging Waters Sacramento

This park has some of the best high-speed slides and other water attractions.

✉ Exposition Boulevard, Sacramento ☎ 916/924-3447; www.rwsac.com 🕒 Late May–early Sep; call for hours 🖐 Expensive

Raging Waters San Jose

The Bay area's only water theme park, with large and long waterslides designed to please. There are over 30 different attractions. Older children will love the innertube rides.

✉ Lake Cunningham Park, 2333 S White Road, San Jose ☎ 408/238-9900; www.rwsplash.com 🕒 May–Sep, call for hours 🖐 Expensive

Six Flags Magic Mountain

Specializing in thrill rides, the park also offers a mini-zoo and the Wizard's Village for younger members of the family. Admission price covers everything but food.

✉ 26101 Magic Mountain Parkway, off Interstate 5 Freeway, near Valencia ☎ 661/255-4103; www.sixflags.com/magicmountain 🕒 Call for hours 🖐 Expensive

Universal Studios

See page 142.

Top nightlife spots

The Blank Club
One of the South Bay's most happening places, especially for live up and coming punk and indie talent.

✉ 44 South Almaden Avenue, San Jose ☎ 408/292-5265; www.theblankclub.com

Cameron's Inn
British-themed pub on the Peninsula coast, featuring fine ales, pub games, TV sports and two double-decker buses.

✉ 1410 South Cabrilo Highway, Half Moon Bay ☎ 650/726-5705; www.cameronsinn.com

The Casbah
The live music is more indie rock than Middle Eastern but the Casbah is one of the most atmospheric venues in town.

✉ 2501 Kettner Boulevard, San Diego ☎ 619/232-4355; www.casbahmusic.com

Dresden Lounge
Attached to the famous eponymous restaurant, the lounge hosts laid-back jazz by Marty and Elaine most nights.

✉ 1760 North Vermont Avenue, Hollywood ☎ 323/665-4294, www.thedresden.com

The End Up
This is one of the city's best places for cutting edge techno and dance music, with forays into reggae and other genres.

✉ 401 6th Street, San Francisco ☎ 415/646-0999; www.theendup.com

Heinhold's First and Last Chance
This tiny wooden saloon with a sloping floor has hardly changed since Jack London used to drink here.

✉ 48 Webster Street, Jack London Square, Oakland ☎ 510/839-6761; www.heinholdsfirstandlastchance.com

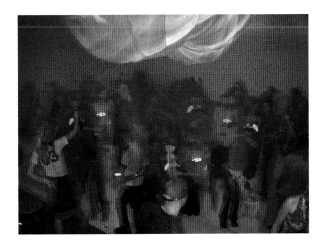

Library Alehouse
This excellent bar offers a huge range of ales from top West Coast microbreweries and organizes fun events.
✉ 2911 Main Street, Santa Monica ☎ 310/314-4855; www.libraryalehouse.com

Little Temple
The oriental decorations add a touch of Zen to this vibrant club, which features a range of live music and DJs.
✉ 4519 Santa Monica Boulevard, Los Angeles ☎ 323/660-4540; www.littletemple.com

Mad Dog in the Fog
Lively gathering place in the Lower Haight for soccer on TV, darts, good beer and merriment.
✉ 530 Haight Street, San Francisco ☎ 415/626-7279

Pub (Schmidt's Trading & Tobacco Co)
A fittingly relaxed and bookish pub on the Berkeley border that supplies ales to academics in armchairs poring over atlases.
✉ 1492 Solano Avenue, Albany ☎ 510/525-1900

Stunning views around LA

Angeles Crest Highway: This vertiginous route through the San Gabriel mountains is surrounded by marvelous scenery on all sides. ✚ 10W

Getty Center: There are grand views of West LA and beyond to be had from the top of this iconic skyscraper (➤ 137).

Griffith Observatory: At the peak of Griffith Park, this observatory allows you to see parts of Hollywood and the San Fernando Valley (➤ 138).

Inspiration Point: This summit within Will Rogers State Historic Park looks out onto Pacific Palisades and the ocean. ✚ 9W

LA City Hall: The Observation Deck on the 27th floor is the best place for a bird's-eye view of downtown LA (➤ 132–133).

Mount Wilson Observatory: Perched on the verdant hills north of Pasadena, the observatory offers a stunning vista. ✚ 10W

Mulholland Drive: Even more famous since having a film named after it, this road winds along the crest of the Hollywood Hills. ✚ 9W

Point Vicente: This viewpoint on the lush Palos Verdes Peninsula southwest of the city has sweeping views. ✚ 9W

Point Dume: You can get an excellent overview of Malibu Beach from this natural vantage point at its southern tip. ✚ 9X

Solstice Canyon: For a great view of Santa Monica Bay take the Deer Valley loop trail up through the canyon. ✚ 9W

Exploring

Describing California and its people is like trying to describe a beautiful painting: most people will have a different perspective and feeling. The word that most readily comes to mind is extreme. Nowhere on earth can one find such *extreme* variances of scenic splendor or inhabitants. Within an 80-mile (129km) span are the highest and lowest elevations in the United States, each with its own unique beauty.

From the very first person to set foot in the state to its most recent émigré, the trait that has most greatly characterized the state's populace is a deep commitment to adventure. California seems to define the concept of diversity with both its geography and its inhabitants. With nearly every culture represented throughout the state, there are enough dining and entertainment selections to suit everyone's desire.

San Francisco

San Francisco

The Gold Rush of the mid-19th century brought a diverse ethnicity to San Francisco. Areas like Chinatown and North Beach have preserved their different native cultures.

Out in the bay to the north is the infamous Alcatraz Island, the site of the notorious former prison. It is easily seen from Coit Tower, on top of Telegraph Hill. Russian Hill provides a panoramic look at the Golden Gate Bridge and the bay. To the north and east of the city lie the Napa Valley and Marin County, where wine-tasting is the hobby of choice.

Few places in the world can boast, as San Francisco can, the sophistication of a major metropolitan area, while also being offset by 42 hills and, at the same time, surrounded by the serenity of lush vineyards.

ALCATRAZ

Of the 14 islands punctuating the massive San Francisco Bay, 12-acre (5ha) Alcatraz is the most famous. Rising 135ft (41m) out of the bay, it is easy to see why it is nicknamed "The Rock." Although wild flowers are abundant on the island and the views of the bay and the Golden Gate bridge are breathtaking, most visitors visit the island to tour the massive fortress that covers most of the grounds. Built in 1858 as a military post, it soon became a military prison and finally a federal penitentiary.

Escape from the prison was reputed to be impossible, due to severe tides and undertow of the surrounding chilly waters. Three inmates dug their way out of their prison cells and disappeared in 1962. No one knows if they made it to the mainland, but their bodies were never found. The prison closed soon after the attempt, and a group of Native Americans claimed the island as their birthright. Some of the buildings were burned before the National Park Service took control and reopened Alcatraz as a tourist attraction in 1973.

Three prominent movies have been filmed on the island: *Escape from Alcatraz*, *The Birdman of Alcatraz* and *The Rock*. Tours include a close-up look at the cells with audio-cassette narration by former prisoners and guards and exterior trail walks led by park rangers. Dress warmly and wear comfortable shoes.

www.alcatrazcruises.com

➕ *San Francisco 2a (off map)* ☎ 415/981-7625 ⏱ Hours vary, advance reservations recommended 💵 Moderate 🚢 Ferry from Pier 33, Fisherman's Wharf

ASIAN ART MUSEUM

More than 40 Asian countries are represented in this museum, the largest of its kind outside the Asian continent. Exclusive to this museum are works of Asian art spanning 4,000 years of Chinese history. It also houses outstanding exhibits from India, Japan and Korea and more than 300 works from the estates of Chinese emperors.

www.asianart.org

➕ *San Francisco 2f* ✉ 200 Larkin Street, Civic Center ☎ 415/581-3500 ⏱ Tue–Sun 10–5 (Feb–Sep Thu until 9) 💵 Moderate; free 1st Tue of month

CABLE CAR MUSEUM AND POWERHOUSE VIEWING GALLERY

If you're fascinated by San Francisco's cable-cars, visit this working nerve center and museum. On exhibit are the first cable-cars, which went unchanged for almost 100 years until modernized in 1982. Also in the red-brick 1907 barn are photographs and a model collection. From the viewing gallery watch craftsmen at work.

www.cablecarmuseum.org

🚏 *San Francisco 3d* ✉ 1201 Mason Street ☎ 415/474-1887 🕐 Daily 10–5 (extended hours in spring and summer) 🎟 Free

CALIFORNIA ACADEMY OF SCIENCES

Dating back to the mid-19th century, this is considered one of the finest natural science museums in the world. It houses several galleries, an exhibit that allows visitors to "experience" an earthquake, and a hands-on Discovery Room for children. The Steinhart Aquarium has almost 14,000 salt-water species that include octopuses, sea-horses, dolphins and sharks. Elsewhere, the Kimball Natural History museum addresses subjects such as

evolution and climate change. Other attractions include the informative and spectacular shows at the Morrison Planetarium, and the hot and humid four-story Rainforests of the World section.
www.calacademy.org

➕ *San Francisco 1f (off map)* ✉ 55 Music Concourse Drive, Golden Gate Park ☎ 415/379-8000 🕓 Mon–Sat 9:30–5, Sun 11–5 (extended hours in summer) 💰 Moderate; senior/children rates; free 3rd Wed of month

CALIFORNIA PALACE OF THE LEGION OF HONOR

Refurbished in 1995, this classical palace was inspired by the Hotel de Salm in Paris, the site where Napoleon established the Legion D'Honneur. The Palace houses an extraordinary collection of 75,000 prints and drawings from the Achenbach Foundation, and expansive European art dating from 2500BC through to the 20th century. Rodin's *The Thinker* is on display in the courtyard.
www.famsf.org

➕ *San Francisco 1d (off map)* ✉ 34th Avenue and Clement Street, Lincoln Park ☎ 415/750-3600 🕓 Tue–Sun 9:30–5 💰 Moderate; free 1st Tue of month

CARTOON ART MUSEUM

This museum houses permanent and rotating exhibits of original two- and three-dimensional art and cartoon artifacts. You can see the original artwork and drawings used in the production of cartoons. Some exhibits go back to the 18th century.

www.cartoonart.org

✚ *San Francisco 4e* ✉ 655 Mission Street ☎ 415/227-8666 🕐 Tue–Sun 11–5. Closed public hols ♿ Inexpensive; senior/children rates

CHINESE HISTORICAL SOCIETY OF AMERICA

The largest collection of Chinese-American artifacts in the US is housed here, including Chinese dragon heads, an 1880 Buddhist altar and a concise history of the Chinese experience in America, from 1840 to the present day.

www.chsa.org

✚ *San Francisco 3d* ✉ 965 Clay Street ☎ 415/391-1188 🕐 Tue–Fri noon–5, Sat 11–4 ♿ Inexpensive

CIVIC CENTER PLAZA

Dominated by the French Renaissance-inspired City Hall, the complex dates back to the 1906 earthquake. On the west end is the War Memorial and Performing Arts Center. The Center is home to the Louise M. Davies Symphony Hall, the War Memorial Opera House and the War Memorial Veterans Building. The latter contains the San Francisco Museum of Modern Art and the Herbst Theatre, where the United Nations charter was signed in 1945. Other classically-styled buildings in the plaza complex are the Civic Auditorium, the San Francisco Public Library and the State Building.

✚ *San Francisco 2f* ✉ Van Ness Avenue/Polk Street at Grove and McAllister streets ☎ 415/557-4266 (information) ♿ Free

DE YOUNG MUSEUM

An extensive collection of American artwork is contained in this complex set in Golden Gate Park; exhibits include paintings,

sculpture, decorative arts, textiles and furniture, some dating to the mid-17th century. Also on display are classical and tribal works.
www.famsf.org

➕ *San Francisco 1f (off map)* ✉ 50 Hagiwara Tea Garden Drive, Golden Gate Park ☎ 415/750-3600 🕐 Tue–Sun 9:30–5:15 (mid-Jan to Nov Fri until 8:45) ✋ Moderate; free 1st Tue of month

FISHERMAN'S WHARF

Bustling Fisherman's Wharf has many shops, street stands, food emporia and the like. Originally, it was an active base for San Francisco Bay's once busy fishing industry, until the late 1940s. A small fleet still operates.

➕ *San Francisco 2a* ✉ North of North Beach 🍴 Cafés, stands ($)

a walk around Chinatown

This walk takes you through the largest Chinese community outside Asia.

Enter through the Chinatown Gate, at Bush Street and Grant Avenue.

Note the dragon-entwined lampposts and pagoda roofs as you are greeted by a cacophony of Chinese street merchants and the aromas of simmering noodles.

Walk north on Grant to the Dragon House Antiques (No 455).

Continue up Grant to St. Mary's Park where there's a 12ft (3.5m) sculpture of Sun Yat-sen.

Continue north to Clay, turn right to Kearny, then left to Portsmouth Square. Across Kearny is the Holiday Inn.

Pop inside to the Chinese Cultural Center.

Go north on Kearny, to Pacific, then turn left. Continue west on Pacific to Grant, then go left two blocks to Washington. Turn left and you will find the Penang Garden restaurant (No 728), a good choice for lunch.

Admire the three-tiered pagoda-style Bank of Canton, then continue west to the Tien Hou Temple (in Waverly Place on Washington). Around the corner is The Great China Herb Co. (No 857), where sellers fill herbal prescriptions.

Double back west on Washington to Stockton, and then turn left.

The Chinese Six Companies building (No 843) is an architectural wonder, with its curved roof tiles and elaborate cornices.

Walk south on Stockton to the Stockton Street Tunnel. A 15-minute walk through the tunnel brings you to downtown Union Square.

Distance 5 miles (8km)
Time 2–4 hours
Start point Chinatown Gate 🚇 *San Francisco 4d*
End point Union Square 🚇 *San Francisco 3e*
Lunch Penang Garden ($$), 728 Washington Street; tel: 415/296-7878

GOLDEN GATE BRIDGE AND NATIONAL RECREATION AREA

Best places to see, ➤ 42–43.

GRACE CATHEDRAL
Taking over a half-century to build, this marvelous structure is a near-perfect replica of a Florentine cathedral. The singing of the choral Evensong each Thursday at 5:15pm is a truly spiritual experience.
www.gracecathedral.org
➕ *San Francisco 2d* ✉ 1100 California Street ☎ 415/749-6300 Donations

HYDE STREET PIER AND HISTORICAL SHIPS

In the Fisherman's Wharf area, this pier is the permanent home of several historical ships. Here you will find the ferry boat *Eureka* (1890), once the world's largest ferry boat, and the *Balclutha*, a square-rigged sailing ship from Scotland (1886), famed for rounding Cape Horn several times. Before leaving the area, drop into the National Maritime Museum at nearby Aquatic Park.

🜨 *San Francisco 1a* ☎ 415/447-5000 🕐 Daily 9:30–5 ✋ Inexpensive. National Park Golden Eagle Pass free

LOMBARD STREET

Located in the Russian Hill district, this is San Francisco's famous "crookedest" street. Traffic zigzags down it at 5mph (8kph), moving around colorful gardens that were established in the 1920s.

🜨 *San Francisco 1b–4b* ✉ Between Hyde and Leavenworth streets

MISSION SAN FRANCISCO DE ASIS

Founded in 1776 and moved to its present site in 1782, the mission is thought to be the oldest standing structure in the city. Adjoining it is the Mission Dolores Basilica, the least changed of all California's existing missions. The architecture of Mission Dolores is a combination of Moorish, Mission and Corinthian styles, and the cemetery is filled with the burial sites of San Francisco pioneers.

www.missiontour.org

✚ *San Francisco 2f (off map)* ✉ 16th and Dolores streets ☎ 415/621-8203
🕐 Daily 9–4:30 (until 4 in fall and winter) 🖐 Inexpensive

NORTH BEACH

This thriving, trendy neighborhood, on the northeastern tip of San Francisco, is bound by Chinatown, the Financial District and Russian Hill. North Beach has a distinctly Italian atmosphere, and is central to most attractions, shops and restaurants in the area. Its heyday in the 1950s saw Jack Kerouac and other Beat Generation poets frequenting the cafés and bookstores, which remain important cultural meeting places. At the center of the neighborhood is **Coit Tower**, an impressive 210ft (64m) landmark, built in 1934, reached on foot via the Filbert Steps by Darnell Place.

✚ San Francisco 3b

Coit Tower

☎ 415/362 0808 ⏰ Daily 10–5 ✋ Inexpensive (to go to top of tower)

PALACE OF FINE ARTS

This Bernard Maybeck Greco-Romanesque rotunda is one of the most photographed buildings in San Francisco. Levelled by the great earthquake of 1906, it was completely rebuilt in 1915 and today presents continuing cultural events. Inside the complex is the Exploratorium, a wonderful hands-on science museum, ideal for families, with toys disguised as science education.

www.exploratorium.edu

✚ San Francisco 1b (off map)

📮 3601 Lyon Street ☎ 415/561-0399 ⏰ Tue–Sun 10–5; open on Mon hols ✋ Moderate; free 1st Wed of month

ST MARY'S CATHEDRAL OF THE ASSUMPTION

The radical architecture by Pietro Belluschi and Pier Luigi Nervi caused great debate during construction. Rising on concrete pylons to a height of 190ft (58m), the exterior resembles a washing machine agitator. Inside, however, the soaring cruciform is breathtaking. The majestic pipe organ, itself, is worth seeing.

✚ San Francisco 1e 📮 1111 Gough Street ☎ 415/567-2020 ⏰ Daily 7–5 ✋ Free, but donations accepted

SAN FRANCISCO MUSEUM OF MODERN ART

Devoted solely to modern art and occupying a quarter-million sq ft, this is the main structure in the Yerba Buena Arts Center (SoMo district). Exhibits include a world-renowned collection of photography, and 20th-century works from such artists as Dali, O'Keefe and Jasper Johns. A feature exhibit is "From Matisse to Diebenkorn: Works from the Permanent Collection."

www.sfmom.org

✚ *San Francisco 4e* ✉ 151 3rd Street ☎ 415/357-4000 🕐 Mon, Tue, Fri–Sun 11–5:45; Thu 11–8:45 ✋ Moderate; senior/student rates; free 1st Tue of month

TRANSAMERICA PYRAMID

Depending on who you ask, this structure is either a landmark or an eyesore. Completed in 1972, the pyramid skyscraper juts 853ft (260m) skyward, making it the tallest building in San Francisco. No public access.

www.thepyramidcenter.com

✚ *San Francisco 4d* ✉ 600 Montgomery Street

UNION STREET

Union Street runs east–west from Montgomery Street in North Beach to the Presidio. It is one of the city's most fashionable areas in which to live and shop, with its many beautifully restored Victorian mansions that have been converted into boutiques, art galleries and cafés. Scattered among the bustling retail spots are several landmarks. The **Octagon House** (just off Union Street) is a pale-blue, eight-sided structure that features antique furniture from the 18th and 19th centuries. Also of interest is an exhibit containing the signatures of 54 of the 56 original signatories of the Declaration of Independence.

✚ San Francisco 2c–4b

Octagon House

✉ 2645 Gough Street ☎ 415/441-7512 🕐 2nd and 4th Thu and 2nd Sun of each month (except Jan) noon–3. Closed public hols 💵 Contributions

WELLS FARGO HISTORY MUSEUM

The Wells Fargo History Museum connects the Wells Fargo Bank's history to the Gold Rush, historic San Francisco and stage coach travel in early California. Henry Wells and William Fargo started Wells Fargo & Co. in 1852, providing express and banking services to the '49ers. Visitors can see an original stage coach and rare gold coins and nuggets, work a telegraph, and learn about the people who built the West.

www.wellsfargo.com

✚ San Francisco 4d ✉ 420 Montgomery Street ☎ 415/396-2619 🕐 Mon–Fri 9–5. Closed public hols 💵 Free

HOTELS

☗☗☗ Columbus Motor Inn ($)
A range of good-value and comfortable rooms and suites, within easy walking distance of Fisherman's Wharf and North Beach.
✉ 1075 Columbus Avenue ☏ 415/885-1492; www.columbusmotorinn.com

☗☗ Comfort Inn by the Bay ($)
Comfortable chain hotel that affords some fine views near Lombard Street and the major attractions. Reasonable rates.
✉ 2775 Van Ness Avenue ☏ 415/928-5000; www.comfortinn.com

☗☗ Cow Hollow Motor Inn ($)
There are spacious but simple rooms and quaint communal areas in this Alpine-style motel with great rates and plenty of parking.
✉ 2190 Lombard Street ☏ 415/921-5800; www.cowhollowmotorinn.com

☗☗☗☗ The Fairmont San Francisco ($$$)
Atop Nobb Hill, this imposing neo-classical building contains luxuriously renovated rooms that offer panoramic city views.
✉ 950 Mason Street ☏ 415/772-5000; www.fairmont.com/sanfrancisco

☗☗☗ Hotel Triton ($$$)
Near Chinatown, the hotel in a tasteful art deco design with exhibitions of local artwork in the lobby. The rooms are stylishly furnished in boutique fashion.
✉ 342 Grant Avenue ☏ 415/394-0500; www.hoteltriton.com

☗☗☗ Hotel Vertigo ($$)
Renovated in 1922 with marble floors and stylish rooms, the hotel is named after the Alfred Hitchcock movie, parts of which were filmed here.
✉ 940 Sutter Street ☏ 415/885-6800; www.yorkhotel.com

☗☗☗ The Inn at the Opera ($$)
Near the Performing Arts Center, an elegant hotel with top service and antique European furniture that adds to the French ambience.
✉ 333 Fulton Street ☏ 415/863-8400; www.shellhospitality.com

▼▼▼ ▼▼▼ Inter-Continental Mark Hopkins ($$)

On the site of the old Mark Hopkins mansion, the hotel offers a spectacular view of the city from its grand location on Nob Hill.

✉ 1 Nob Hill ☎ 415/392-3434; www.intercontinental.com

▼▼▼ Mill Valley Inn ($$)

Beautiful stucco hotel at the center of this small, artistic community in beautiful Marin County, on the north side of the Golden Gate Bridge.

✉ 165 Throckmorton Avenue, Mill Valley ☎ 415/389-6608; www.jdvhotels.com

▼▼▼ Sir Francis Drake ($$)

The British Empire theme is accentuated by a dazzling display of heraldry in the magnificently restored lobby, while the bedrooms are painted a calmer green.

✉ 450 Powell Street ☎ 415/392-7755; www.sirfrancisdrake.com

RESTAURANTS

▼▼▼ Alfred's Steakhouse ($$)

Since 1928 hungry San Franciscans have been feasting on huge portions of red meat in a quaint bordello-like environment.

✉ 659 Merchant Street, between Kearny and Montgomery streets
☎ 415/781-7058; www.alfredssteakhouse.com 🕐 Tue, Wed, Fri and Sat 5:30–9:30, Thu 11:30–2

▼▼▼ Aziza ($$$)

Only local and organic ingredients make up the menu at this cutting-edge establishment. There's a 5-course tasting menu.

☎ 5800 Geary Boulevard ☎ 415/752-2222; www.aziza-sf.com
🕐 Wed–Mon 5:30–10

▼▼▼ Balboa Cafe ($$)

The traditional American menu with a nouveau California twist includes the likes of Estancia grass-fed New York steak.

✉ 3199 Fillmore Street ☎ 415/921-3944; www.balboacafe.com 🕐 Sun–Tue 11:30–9, Wed–Sat 11:30–10

☗☗ Betelnut ($$)

A lively atmosphere sets the scene for tropical drinks and pan-Asian fare with elements of Thai, Chinese and Korean cuisine.

✉ 2030 Union Street ☎ 415/929-8855; www.betelnutrestaurant.com
🕙 Sun–Thu 11:30–11, Fri and Sat 11:30–midnight

☗☗☗ Bix ($$$)

Martinis, cigar smoke, an upscale crowd and great steaks and seafood make this one of San Francisco's most popular restaurants. Reservations recommended.

✉ 56 Gold Street, between Montgomery and Sansome streets ☎ 415/433-6300; www.bixrestaurant.com 🕙 Sat–Thu 5:50–10, Fri 11:30–2, 5:50–10

☗☗ Borobudur ($$)

The names of the dishes are as exotic as the flavors at this great Indonesian restaurant; you could always try the set menu.

✉ 700 Post Street ☎ 415/775-1512; www.borobudursf.com 🕙 Mon–Thu 11:30–10, Fri–Sat 11:30–11, Sun 1–10

☗☗ Brenda's French Soul Food ($)

New Orleans-style diner popular for breakfast brunch and lunch, serving French and Creole dishes such as fried oyster po-boy.

✉ 658 Polk Street ☎ 415/345-8100: www.frenchsoulfood.com
🕙 Daily 8–3

☗☗☗ Le Charm ($$)

French bistro and garden for indoor or outdoor dining, with terrific prix-fixe menu. The braised veal *paupiette* is a good choice.

✉ 315 5th Street ☎ 415/546-6128; www.lecharm.com 🕙 Tue–Fri 11:30–3, 5:30–9:30, Sat 5:30–10, Sun 5–8:30

☗☗ Dosa on Valencia ($$)

This establishment specializes in *dosas* – elongated south Indian rice pancakes, stuffed with vegetables and accompanied by spicy sauces.

✉ 995 Valencia Street ☎ 415/642-3672: www.dosasf.com 🕙 Mon–Fri 5:30–10, Sat–Sun 11:30–3:30, 5:30–10

₩₩ Dottle's True Blue Cafe ($)
See page 58.

₩₩ ₩₩ Fleur de Lys ($$$)
The city's most romantic restaurant offering attentive service and superb contemporary French food. Don't miss the delicious liquer souffles.

✉ 777 Sutter Street ☎ 415/673-7779; www.fleurdelyssf.com 🕐 Tue–Thu 6–9:30, Fri 5:30–10:30, Sat 10–10:30

₩₩ Fog City Diner ($$)
Upscale 50s-style diner on Telegraph Hill where you can sample American and seafood specialties such as slow roasted Hereford beef short rib and sautéed Arctic char.

✉ 1300 Battery Street ☎ 415/982-2000; www.fogcitydiner.com
🕐 Mon–Thu 11:30–10, Fri 11:30–11, Sat 10:30–11, Sun 10:30–10

₩₩₩ Gary Danko ($$$)
Romantic Russian Hill/wharf restaurant featuring an exciting mix of French–Californian fare. Diners can design their own three- to five-course meal. Pricey, but worth it.

✉ 800 N Point Street ☎ 415/749-2060; www.garydanko.com 🕐 Daily 5:30–10

₩₩ Izakaya Sozai ($$)
Japanese tapas bar serving quality Japanese dishes, from sashimi and yakitori to entrées such as whole fried squid, plus a range of sake.

✉ 1500 Irving Street ☎ 415/742-5122: www.izakayasozai.com
🕐 Sun–Mon, Wed–Thu 5:30–10, Sat–Sun 5:30–11

₩₩ Limón ($)
Lots of great tastes come out of this Peruvian rotisserie with an emphasis on roast chicken but also a line in empanadas and ceviches.

✉ 1001 South Van Ness Avenue ☎ 415/821-2134; www.limonrotisserie.com
🕐 Daily 11–11

EXPLORING

☗☗☗ Lu Lu ($$)

Innovative, Mediterranean bistro located in a large converted warehouse. Family-style service with excellent food.

✉ 816 Folsom ☏ 415/495-5775; www.restaurantlulu.com 🕔 Daily 11:30–11

☗ Mijita ($)

Conveniently located Mexican joint, where you can feast cheaply on tasty tacos and other spicy favorites.

✉ 1 Ferry Building ☏ 415/399-0814; www.mijitasf.com 🕔 Mon–Thu 10–7, Fri 10–8, Sat 9–8, Sun 10–4

☗☗ Pork Store Café ($)

A local institution for filling breakfasts and lunches, from omelettes and pancakes to succulent burgers.

✉ 1451 Haight Street ☏ 415/864-6981; www.porkstorecafe.com 🕔 Mon–Fri 7–3:30, Sat–Sun 8–4

SHOPPING

ART AND ANTIQUES
Fillmore Street

Specialty shops include book and music stores, and clothing from retro to new fashion.

✉ Jackson and Sutter ☏ www.fillmoreshop.com

The Japan Center

Art galleries and Oriental gift shops, interspersed with sushi bars and tea houses.

✉ Bounded by Laguna, Geary, Fillmore, Sutter and Post streets
☏ www.sfjapantown.org

CRAFTS
Fisherman's Wharf

There are four shopping centers at Fisherman's Wharf – Pier 39, The Cannery, Ghirardelli Square and The Anchorage to keep keen shoppers satisfied. See also page 63.

✉ Columbus on the Bay ☏ www.fishermanswharf.org

FASHION
Haight Street
Famous for hippies in the 1960s; some shops still sell offbeat, vintage clothes. Book and music shops also feature here.

✉ At Ashbury Street

Union Square
Large department stores are Macy's, Neiman-Marcus and Saks Fifth Avenue.

✉ Downtown ☎ Macy's 415/397-3333; Neiman-Marcus 415/362-3900; Saks Fifth Avenue 415/986-4300; www.unionsquareshop.com

Union Street
One of the best streets in San Francisco, with specialist shops/galleries.

✉ Between Gough and Steiner ☎ www.unionstreet.com

STORES
The Embarcadero Center
Shops, restaurants, offices and hotels all housed in a huge downtown complex.

✉ Sacramento and Clay streets ☎ www.embarcaderocenter.com

Ghirardelli Square
Formerly a chocolate factory, this area has become a chic center of stores and top restaurants.

✉ At Fisherman's Wharf ☎ www.ghirardellisq.com

ENTERTAINMENT

PERFORMING ARTS
American Conservatory Theater (ACT)
One of the top regional theaters in the US.

✉ 415 Geary Street ☎ 415/749-2228; www.act-sf.org

Louise M. Davies Symphony Hall
Guided tours are available of this stream-lined glass-and-granite building that hosts epic symphonies and concerts and which is

home to the San Francisco Symphony.

✉ Van Ness Avenue and Grove Street, Civic Center ☎ 415/864-6000;
www.sfwmpac.org

Magic Theatre
Cutting edge theater that showcases contemporary playwrights
such as Sam Shepard and up-and-coming new talent.
✉ Fort Mason Center, Building D, Fort Mason ☎ 415/441-8822;
www.magictheatre.org

Orpheum Theater
The largest touring shows to San Francisco play here.
✉ 1192 Market Street ☎ 415/551-2000; www.orpheum-theater.com

War Memorial Opera House
Home to the highly respected San Francisco Opera company, the
imposing 1932 structure is a cultural institution in its own right.
✉ 301 Van Ness Avenue ☎ 415/864-3330; www.sfopera.org

NIGHTLIFE
Bottom of the Hill
Alternative bands head to this Potrero Hill club, which has a beer
garden, pool tables and also serves food.
✉ 1233 17th Street ☎ 415/621-4455; www.bottomofthehill.com

The End Up
See page 70.

Ruby Skye
One of the city's most buzzing nightclubs, which hosts all the top
dance and techno DJs, as well as live acts.
✉ 420 Mason Street ☎ 415/693-0777; www.rubyskye.com

Vesuvio Cafe
This former haunt of Beat poets hasn't changed much in the 30
years since it opened to doors.
✉ 255 Columbus Avenue ☎ 415/362-3370; www.vesuvio.com

Northern California

Sacramento

Some of California's most beautiful areas can be found in the north of the state. Majestic Mount Shasta and Lassen Volcanic National Park epitomize the sheer grandeur of nature, while San Francisco, with its rich cultural diversity, is its most attractive city.

Yosemite National Park, Lake Tahoe and the Wine Country all share qualities of untouched beauty. The northern coastline is the least populated and is a

perfect contrast to the busy beach areas to the south. Nowhere can you find natural beauty like that of the Redwood National Forest, which is said to contain the world's tallest tree.

Silicon Valley, south of San Francisco, is the center of the country's computer and electronics industries, and Sacramento is the state capital and center of government.

EUREKA

Eureka is the largest town on California's northernmost coast. Set along Humboldt Bay, it is home to an impressive fishing fleet. Its name, from the Greek word for "I have found it," refers to the cries from many gold miners (called '49ers) in the 19th century. The Old Town section has elegant Victorian homes.

The old 1912 building, once the town's main bank, now houses the **Clarke Memorial Museum,** which features a collection of California Native American historic artifacts.

Blue Ox Millworks is a working mill that includes a blacksmith shop and a re-creation of a logging camp. **Sequoia Park Zoo,** a beautiful grove of virgin redwoods in 52 acres (21ha), has a formal flower garden, duck pond, and deer and elk paddocks, plus other animals.

🚫 2C

Clarke Memorial Museum

✉ 240 E Street ☎ 707/443-947; www.clarkemuseum.org ⏰ Wed–Sat 11–4 ✋ Free

Blue Ox Millworks

✉ Foot of X Street ☎ 707/444-3437; www.blueoxmill.com ⏰ Mon–Fri 9–5 ✋ Inexpensive

Sequoia Park Zoo

✉ 3414 W Street ☎ 707/442-6552; www.sequoiaparkzoo.com ⏰ Jun–Aug daily 10–5; Sep–May Tue–Sun 10–5 ✋ Inexpensive 🍴 Picnic facilities

GOLD COUNTRY TOWNS

Also known as the Mother Lode Country, this scenic area extends 300 miles (484km) along Highway 49, through the western Sierra

Nevada foothills. Once the thriving Old West, it is now mostly ghost towns, several of which are open to tourists.

Angel's Camp Museum, in Angel's Camp (➤ 102), was the center for gravel and quartz mining in 1849. You can see photographs, relics and 3 acres (1.21ha) of mining equipment from the old days.

Marshall Gold Discovery State Historic Park is where James Marshall discovered gold. The drive-through park features a replica of Sutter's Mill and memorial statue and grave site of James Marshall.

The Empire Mine State Historic Park (➤ 103), 2 miles (3.5km) east of Grass Valley, is the Gold Country's best preserved quartz mining operation. During the boom years, the 367 miles (592km) of mine shafts produced six million ounces of gold.

Mercer Caverns, 1 mile (1.6km) north of Murphys, were discovered in 1885 by gold prospector Walter Mercer. The 45-minute tour gives the opportunity to view the huge stalagmites and stalactites close up.

➕ 6G

Angel's Camp Museum
✉ 753 South Main Street ☎ 209/736-2963; www.angelscamp.gov 🕐 Mar–Dec Thu–Mon 10–4; Jan–Feb Sat–Sun 10–4 💲 Inexpensive

Marshall Gold Discovery State Historic Park
✉ South fork of the American River and Highway 49, Coloma ☎ 530/622-3470; www.parks.ca.gov 🕐 Museum Mar–Oct Tue–Sun 10–4; Nov–Feb 10–3; park daily 8–sunset 💲 Inexpensive

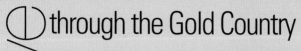

through the Gold Country

This drive will take you through the glorious Gold Country, along the historic Highway 49 through what was once the thriving Old West.

Begin this scenic tour in Mariposa, where SR 49 meets SR 140.

Here you can visit the California State Mining and Mineral Museum and the Mariposa County Museum.

Proceed north on SR 49 to Chinese Camp and the State Historic Park. A few miles north is Jamestown.

Jamestown served as a backdrop for the film *High Noon* and the television series *Little House on the Prairie*.

Follow 49 north, stopping in Tuttletown.

You can view a replica of Mark Twain's cabin on Jackass Hill (Tuttletown was originally called Jackass Gulch).

Continue to Columbia.

Here you can try your hand at panning for gold, or ride an authentic stagecoach.

Continue north on 49 to Angel's Camp.

This is where Mark Twain first heard the "jumping frog" story from bartender Ben Coon. If you are here in May, don't miss the frog jumping contest. The foundation of Angel's Mine is across from the Catholic Church.

Continue north to Jackson and Placerville.

Jackson was formerly home of the Mohawk Indians, and Placerville was once known as "Hangtown."

Farther north are Coloma, Auburn and Grass Valley.

The latter is home to Empire Mine State Historic Park and North Star Mine Museum, both offering tours.

The drive ends in Nevada City.

Distance Approximately 100 miles (162km)
Time 8 hours
Start point Mariposa ✚ 7R
End point Nevada City ✚ 5E
Lunch National Hotel Restaurant ($$), 18183 Main Street, Jamestown; tel: 209/984-3446; www.national-hotel.com

LAKE TAHOE

Situated on the California–Nevada stateline, Lake Tahoe is one of the most popular resort communities in the state. Although this beautiful lake is 6,228ft (1,899m) above sea level, it never freezes because of its depth. You will find the very best ski facilities here, and in summer, watersports include lake cruises, water skiing and sailing.

For a spectacular aerial view of the entire area, including the site of the 1960 Winter Olympic Games, ride the gondola to the top of the Squaw Valley Ski Area.

➕ 7N

Squaw Valley Cable Car

✉ 1960 Squaw Valley Road, Olympic Valley ☎ 530/583-6985; www.squaw.com 🕐 Call or check online; closed mid-Oct to Dec 1 💷 Expensive

LASSEN VOLCANIC NATIONAL PARK

Lassen Park stretches over 100,000 acres (40,486ha) in the northeastern corner of California, where the Cascade and Sierra Nevada mountains meet. Highlights are Lassen Peak, Cinder Cone, Prospect Peak and Mount Harkness, the latter two volcanoes topped by cinder cones.

Lassen's numerous volcanic eruptions subsided in 1921 and have been replaced by hot springs and lakes, lava flows and mudpots, all linked together by hiking trails that lead to the summit and back.

➕ 5C ✉ 9 miles (15km) east of Mineral, via SR 36 ☎ 530/595-4444 🕐 Year-round 👋 Moderate

MAMMOTH LAKES RECREATION AREA

This giant popular resort area in the Inyo National Forest has world-class skiing, and in summertime it's a mountain biking mecca. There is also good camping, fishing and horseback riding here. Hike to the 101ft (31m) Rainbow Falls, or visit the Devil's Postpile National Monument, 60ft (18m) multisided columns that are by-products of former volcanic activity.

www.mammothlakes.com

➕ 9Q 🍽 Restaurants ($$) ℹ Chamber of Commerce, tel: 760/934-2712

MENDOCINO

Mendocino, off scenic US 1, is perhaps the most charming small town in California. It is noted for its Cape Cod and Victorian-style architecture and its active, artistic community. The entire town is on the National Register of Historic Places. Film buffs will recognize it from such films as *The Summer of '42*, *East of Eden* and television's *Murder She Wrote*. The Art Center is the epicenter of the many art museums in the community, and includes galleries, live theater and arts and craft fairs.

www.mendocinocoast.com

➕ 2E

Mendocino Art Center

✉ 45200 Little Lake Street ☎ 707/937-5818 or 800/653-3328; www.mendocinoartcenter.org 🕐 Daily 10–5 ✋ Moderate

ℹ Mendocino Chamber of Commerce, 217 South Main Street, Fort Bragg; tel: 707/961-6300; daily 10–4

MODESTO

This quintessential California town was made famous by George Lucas's film *American Graffiti*. Near the center of the state, it is the home of the Blue Diamond Almonds company.

The **McHenry Museum** re-creates a 19th-century school, blacksmith shop, kitchen, country store and others with changing exhibits. The **McHenry Mansion,** a block away, exhibits antique furnishings and artwork in a restored Victorian home.

➕ 5H

McHenry Museum & Mansion

✉ 1402 "I" Street ☎ 209/577-5235 (museum); 209/577-5344 (mansion); www.mchenrymuseum.org 🕐 Tue–Sun noon–4; closed major hols ✋ Free, donations requested ❓ Call to arrange tour of the mansion

MOUNT SHASTA

Spiritual-minded Californians flock to this mountain because it is said to be a "vortex of spiritual energy." For the more earthbound there is hiking, climbing, and skiing in winter. Several surrounding lakes offer waterside camping, fishing and watersports, including skating in winter. The **Mount Shasta State Fish Hatchery,** in the center of the area, produces 5 to 10 million trout annually to stock Northern California lakes.

www.mtshastachamber.com

➕ 4B

Mount Shasta State Fish Hatchery

☎ 530/926-2215 🕐 Daily 7am–dusk 💲 Free

ℹ Chamber of Commerce Visitors Bureau, 300 Pine Street; tel: 800/926-4865; May–Sep Mon–Sat 9–5:30, Sun 9–4:30; Oct–Apr daily 10–4

NAPA VALLEY

Best places to see, ➤ 50–51.

NATURAL BRIDGES STATE BEACH

Set in 65 acres (26ha), this beach, just before Santa Cruz, is a wonderful place to observe the migration of the colorful monarch butterfly between mid-October and February. There are also tide pools to explore, as well as ecological and wildlife exhibits in the visitor center.

🚩 4J ✉ West Cliff Drive ☎ 831/423-4609 🕐 Beach daily 8–dusk; visitor center 10–4 👱 Inexpensive

OAKLAND

Linked to San Francisco by the Bay Bridge, Oakland has long suffered from its close proximity to the city across the bay. In

reality, it is a culturally rich and diversified town and has counted among its famous citizens Jack London and Gertrude Stein. **Oakland Museum** has an extensive collection of historical and contemporary art housed in the Gallery of California Art. The museum is one of the best in the state for studying the diverse cultural make-up and subsequent historical progress.

Lake Merritt, created in the late 19th century by the damming of a section of the Oakland estuary, was one of the first natural wildlife preserves established in the US.

🔒 4H

Oakland Museum

✉ 10th and Oak Street ☎ 510/238-2200; www.museumca.org 🕐 Wed, Sat–Sun 11–5, Thu–Fri 11–8 ✋ Moderate; free 1st Sun of month

PETALUMA

Petaluma is another one of the quintessential small California towns. Situated on the Petaluma River, it has retained most of its 19th-century architecture and, like Modesto (➤ 106), has become a favorite for filming television series and movies. *American Graffiti* and *Peggy Sue Got Married* were both filmed here.

Philanthropist Andrew Carnegie endowed $12,500 toward the construction of the **Historical Museum/Library** in 1903. It houses permanent and rotating exhibits of early 19th-century Petaluma.

🔒 3G

Petaluma Historical Museum/Library

✉ 20 4th Street ☎ 707/778-4398; www.petalumamuseum.com 🕐 Thu–Sat 10–4, Sun noon–3 ✋ Inexpensive

REDWOOD NATIONAL PARK

Best places to see, ➤ 52–53.

SACRAMENTO

Sacramento was once a major supply center for the California '49ers (gold seekers); now it is the state capital. The names of 5,822 Californians killed in the Vietnam War are engraved on the 22 black granite panels of the California Vietnam Veterans Memorial, near the State Capitol Park.

The exquisite **Governor's Mansion** dates from the 1800s and is now a museum of Victoriana. Items from former governors include a 1902 Steinway piano and Persian carpets.

The Historic Paddlewheeler *Spirit of Sacramento* is available for a Sacramento River cruise or special events. The boat's murder-mystery trips are especially popular.

A million-dollar gold collection, ethnic photos and a historic print shop are just some of the items in the five separate areas of the **Sacramento History Museum.** The **California State Railroad Museum** has three entire floors devoted to railroad-related exhibits, including train cars and 21 locomotives.

Noted for its 210ft (64m) dome, the **State Capitol** building is nearly 150 years old, and is open daily for tours. Adobe-style **Sutter's Fort** was the first European outpost in California and contains some interesting period relics.

Other attractions worth visiting while you are in town are **Sacramento Zoo**, which has a large reptile display and 350 species of wild animals, the Raging Waters Sacramento (➤ 69) and Towe Ford Museum.

✚ 5G

Governor's Mansion State Historic Park

✉ 16th and "H" streets ☎ 916/323-3047; www.parks.ca.gov 🕐 Daily 10–4
👆 Inexpensive

Spirit of Sacramento

✉ Old Sacramento's "L" Street Landing ☎ 800/433-0263 🕐 Cruises: lunch, brunch, happy hour, dinner, sunset and sightseeing 👆 Moderate–expensive
🍴 Dinner, brunch and happy hour cruises available

Sacramento History Museum

✉ 101 "I" Street ☎ 916/808-7059 🕐 Daily 10–5 👆 Inexpensive

California State Railroad Museum

✉ 111 "I" Street ☎ 916/445-6645; www.csrmf.org 🕐 Daily 10–5
👆 Inexpensive

State Capitol

✉ Between 10th, 15th, "L" and "N" streets ☎ 916/324-0333;
www.capitolmuseum.ca.gov 🕐 Tours Mon–Fri 8–5, Sat–Sun 9–5 👆 Free

Sutter's Fort Historic Park

✉ 27th and "L" streets ☎ 916/445-4422 🕐 Daily 10–5 👆 Inexpensive

Sacramento Zoo

✉ 3930 Westland Park Drive ☎ 916/264-5885; www.saczoo.com 🕐 Feb–Oct daily 9–4; Nov–Jan 10–4 👆 Moderate

SAN JOSE

San Jose is the 10th largest city in the US. It was founded in the last quarter of the 18th century as El Pueblo de San Jose, and is the oldest Spanish civilian settlement. From 1849 to 1851 it served as the state's capital.

Kelley Park, apart from being a popular city park with such attractions as Happy Hollow family play area and zoo, it also contains the Japanese Friendship Garden and Teahouse and the San Jose Historical Museum.

Babylonian, Sumerian and Assyrian artifacts, mummies, sculptures and more can be found at the **Rosicrucian Egyptian**

Museum and Planetarium. There is also a contemporary art gallery.

The **Winchester Mystery House,** a Victorian mansion and home of eccentric firearms heiress Sarah Winchester, was designed to confuse evil spirits. The layout of the house is so complex, with blind closets, secret passageways, 13 bathrooms and 40 staircases, that even Sarah herself needed a map to find her way around. Over looking the Santa Clara Valley from the 4,209ft (1,283m) summit of Mount Hamilton is the **Lick Observatory.**

➕ 4J

Kelley Park

✉ Senter and Story roads 🕐 Daily 8am to 30 mins before dusk 🍴 Picnic facilities 💷 Inexpensive

Rosicrucian Egyptian Museum and Planetarium

✉ 1342 Naglee Avenue ☎ 408/947-3636; www.eqyptianmuseum.org 🕐 Mon–Thu 9–5, Fri 9–8, Sat–Sun 11–6 💷 Inexpensive

Winchester Mystery House

✉ 525 S Winchester Boulevard ☎ 408/247-2101 🕐 Summer daily 9–7; winter 9–5 💷 Expensive

Lick Observatory

✉ Mount Hamilton Road ☎ 408/274-5061; www.ucolick.org 🕐 Mon–Fri 12:30–5, Sat–Sun 10–5 💷 Free 🍴 No nearby food or auto services

SAUSALITO

This is the first small town in Marin County after crossing the Golden Gate Bridge. Once a fishing town, it has unfortunately been overrun with tacky tourist shops and no longer has the great charm of years past.

➕ 3H ✉ 5 miles (8km) north of San Francisco ⛴ Ferry from Ferry Building or Fisherman's Wharf

WINE COUNTRY

North of San Francisco lie some of the most lush valleys in all of California, the best known of which are the Napa (➤ 50–51) and Sonoma Valleys. It is here that California's vintners tend their grape vines and produce the many varied wines known and enjoyed worldwide. Whether you are driving, bicycling, taking the Wine Train or flying over the area in one of the many hot air balloons that offer spectacular views of the verdant, rolling, wine lands, you will never forget your excursion to the Wine Country.

The estates of the wineries are incredible to see. Take one of the guided tours of the processing facilities with their informative, enticing tastings. While the large wineries are the most popular, don't pass up the small, family-owned ones, of which there are many. Most have wines that rival the greats, with more convivial atmospheres.

The **Napa Valley Wine Train** provides daily excursions through the Napa Valley. The 1917 Pullman Dining Car relives the gracious era of elegant rail travel and distinguished service and makes you feel as if you're riding the Orient Express as the three-hour, 36-mile (58km) trip between Napa and St. Helena allows for a leisurely brunch, lunch or dinner. Many concerns are aired by residents that the wineries are a bit too commercial for the area, but there are rarely complaints from the visitors.

To the west, the Sonoma Valley runs for 15 miles (24km) and is a bit less populated than the Napa Valley. As a rule, the 45 or so wineries here offer more personalized tours, with free tastings and a more relaxed atmosphere. The town of Sonoma itself is a good place to start if you wish to visit the valley. The other center of activity is Santa Rosa, to the north of the region. The Sonoma

Valley is particularly rich in Spanish and Mexican history, so be sure to take note of the area's beautiful architecture.

If you're looking for souvenirs, the on-site gift shops have superb wines they will ship anywhere in the world. The wineries listed are just some of the ones you'll want to explore. *Spotlight's Wine Guide* is a complete guide to the area (☎ 415/898-7908).

✚ 4G

🛈 Napa Valley, 1310 Napa Town Center, Napa; tel: 707/226-7459; www.napavalley.com. Sonoma Valley, 453 1st Street E, Sonoma; tel: 707/996-1090; www.sonomavalley.com

Napa Valley Wine Train

✉ 1275 McKinstry Street, Napa ☎ 707/253-2111 or 800/427-4124; www.winetrain.com 🕔 Year-round ✋ Expensive, reservations and deposit required

Beringer Vineyards

Beringer was one of the first wineries to open its doors to visitors. The staff here are attentive and knowledgeable in discussing the process of wine-making and its history. Regular daily tours.
www. beringer.com

✉ North of downtown St. Helena, 2000 Main Street ☎ 707/963-7115
🕔 Tastings daily 10–5/6; tour times vary ✋ Moderate–expensive

Buena Vista Carneros

As the site of the first vineyard in the valley, Buena Vista, 2 miles (3km) northeast of Sonoma straddling the southern-most tips of

Sonoma and Napa counties, has become a historical landmark.
Hungarian Count Agoston Haraszthy planted the first vines, and
the wine cellars, built in 1857, are the oldest stone cellars in the
state. The Tasting Room offers a selection of award-winning wines
and there is a gift shop, a picnic area, an artists' gallery, self-guided
tours and historical presentations.

www.buenavistacarneros.com

✉ 18000 Old Winery Road, Sonoma ☎ 707/938-1266 🕑 Daily 10–5
✋ Moderate

Kenwood Vineyards

Operating on Jack London's former ranch since 1970, this Sonoma
country winery produces Cabernet Sauvignon, Zinfandel,
Sauvignon Blanc, Chardonnay, Gewürztraminer, Merlot and Pinot
Noir on the estate, which is about an hour's drive north of San
Francisco. Visitors are welcome to sample up to four wines,
which are produced from grapes grown on site and sourced
from local vineyards, and they can hike and take bicycle rides
around the property.

www.kenwoodvineyards.com

✉ 9592 Sonoma Highway (Highway 12), Kenwood ☎ 707/833-5891
🕑 Daily 10–4:30 ✋ Moderate

YOSEMITE NATIONAL PARK

Best places to see, ▶ 54–55.

HOTELS

EUREKA
🔻🔻🔻 Best Western plus Humboldt Bay Inn ($)

Nicely remodeled rooms with a dash of color, handily located for the nightlife of Old Town and getting out into the redwoods.

✉ 232 W 5th Street ☎ 707/443-2234; www.bestwestern.com

LAKE TAHOE
🔻🔻🔻 Best Western Station House Inn ($$)

Central to the lake, with spacious grounds and comfortable rooms. It's close to all the southern shore leisure activities and restaurants.

✉ 901 Park Avenue, South Lake Tahoe ☎ 530/542-1101; www.stationhouseinn.com

MAMMOTH LAKES
🔻🔻🔻 Mammoth Mountain Inn ($$)

Resort complex with free transportation to the ski areas. Horseback riding and hiking/hunting trails are on offer.

✉ 1 Minaret Road ☎ 760/934-2581; www.mammothmountain.com

MENDOCINO
🔻🔻🔻 Headlands Inn Bed & Breakfast ($$)

Remodeled 1868 Victorian establishment with seven rooms and one private cottage. The whole building is elegantly furnished and the lush grounds are delightful.

✉ 14053 Howard and Albion streets ☎ 707/937-4431; www.headlandsinn.com

MOUNT SHASTA
🔻🔻🔻 Best Western Tree House Motor Inn ($)

There are terrific views of the mountain and excellent skiing in the winter. The rooms and lobby have a clean, crisp Alpine feel.

✉ 111 Morgan Way ☎ 530/926-3101; www.bestwestern.com

REDWOOD FOREST
🔻🔻🔻 Benbow Inn ($$)

Lakeside mock-Tudor mansion built in 1926, surrounded by mighty redwoods, is decorated in Victorian style. Rooms have lovely patios.

✉ 445 Lake Benbow Drive, Garberville ☎ 707/923-2124;
www.benbowinn.com 🕐 Closed Jan–Mar

SACRAMENTO
ᵺᵺᵺ Hyatt Regency ($$)
Conveniently located downtown, near the Capitol Building, this
sleek modern establishment even includes hypo-allergenic rooms.
✉ 1209 "L" Street ☎ 916/443-1234; www.sacramento.hyatt.com

SANTA CRUZ
ᵺᵺᵺ Sea & Sand Inn ($$)
Excellent value, considering its location beside the Pacific. All
rooms enjoy ocean views and the suites have hot tubs and patios.
✉ 201 W Cliff Drive ☎ 831/427-3400; www.santacruzmotels.com

WINE COUNTRY
ᵺᵺᵺᵺ Fairmont Sonoma Mission Inn and Spa ($$$)
Exclusive spa in the Spanish-mission style. The grounds are
spectacular and the luxury rooms as lavish as you'd expect.
✉ 100 Boyes Boulevard, Sonoma Highway, Sonoma ☎ 707/938-9000;
www.fairmont.com/sonoma

ᵺᵺᵺ Harvest Inn ($$$)
A small English mock-Tudor inn surrounded by vineyards, where
many rooms have fireplaces and antique furnishings.
✉ One Main Street, St. Helena ☎ 707/963-9463; www.harvestinn.com

ᵺᵺᵺ Silverado Resort ($$$)
Massive resort whose main building resembles a neoclassical
mansion. Facilities include two golf courses and a spa.
✉ 1600 Atlas Peak Road, Napa ☎ 707/257-0200; www.silveradoresort.com

YOSEMITE
ᵺᵺᵺ The Cottages at Tenaya Lodge ($$)
Rustic elegance on the river, with cookouts and wagon rides; but
there's nothing rustic about the superbly furnished rooms.
✉ 1122 Highway 41 ☎ 559/683-6555; www.tenayalodge.com

RESTAURANTS

EAST BAY
☷☷☷ Bay Wolf ($$)
Another fine California cuisine restaurant, with Mediterranean and
Asian touches. Try the Liberty Ranch duck breast.
✉ 3853 Piedmont Avenue, Oakland ☎ 510/655-6004; www.baywolf.com
🕐 Tue–Fri 11:30–2, 5:30–11, Sat–Sun 5:30–11

☷☷☷☷ Chez Panisse ($$$)
Famed as the place where Alice Waters invented California cuisine,
the top-notch, fixed-price menu still changes every day.
✉ 1517 Shattuck Avenue, Berkeley ☎ 510/548-5525; www.chezpanisse.com
🕐 Mon–Sat 6–11

EUREKA
☷☷ Sea Grill ($$)
Extensive seafood menu that includes cod Louisiana and Hawaiian
mahi-mahi. Also great clam chowder and a varied salad bar.
✉ 316 "E" Street, Old Town ☎ 707/443-7187 🕐 Mon–Sat noon–2, 5–9

GOLD COUNTRY
☷☷☷ Sequoia ($$)
Rustic charm and casual elegance combine here. Specialties are a
range of steaks, other meats and some fish dishes.
✉ 643 Bee Street, Placerville ☎ 530/622-5222; www.sequoiaplacerville.
com 🕐 Tue–Thu 4:30–9, Fri–Sat 11:30–10, Sun 9:30–9

MENDOCINO
☷☷ Mendocino Hotel Victorian Dining Room ($$$)
Cozy, antique-filled hotel. Dine in an elegant Victorian parlor or
garden café. Excellent Continental cuisine and seafood specialties.
✉ 45080 Main Street ☎ 707/937-0511; www.mendocinohotel.com
🕐 Sun–Thu 6–9, Fri–Sat 6–9:30

WINE COUNTRY
☷☷ Black Bear Diner ($)
This popular West Coast diner chain allows you to eat inexpensive

breakfasts or filling meals, such as liver, bacon and mash. Note the
signature bear carvings.

✉ 303 Soscal Avenue, Napa ☎ 707/255-2345; www.blackbeardiner.com

🕐 Daily 8am–2am

☆☆☆ The French Laundry ($$$)

Thomas Keller's famed French restaurant takes reservations
months in advance. Try to get a seat in the outdoor dining area.
Prices are very steep.

✉ 6640 Washington Street, Yountville ☎ 707/944-2380;
www.frenchlaundry.com 🕐 Daily 5:30–9:15 (also 11–1 Fri–Sun)

☆☆☆ The Girl & the Fig ($$)

Oozing class from its antique bar to elegant dining room, this place
specializes in well-balanced California cuisine *plats du jour*.

✉ 110 W Spain Street, Sonoma ☎ 707/938-3634;
www.thegirlandthefig.com 🕐 Daily 11:30–10

SHOPPING

FACTORY OUTLETS
Mammoth Luxury Outlets

There are only 10 stores here, but they are some of the best, with
names like Ralph Lauren and Bass.

✉ 3343 Main Street, Mammoth Lakes ☎ 760/934-9771; www.luxuryoutlets.com

Petaluma Village Premium Outlet

Expect to find 50 stores from Saks to Coach to Gap.

✉ 2200 Petaluma Boulevard, Petaluma ☎ 707/778-9300;
www.premiumoutlets.com

GIFTS
David Berkley Collection

Eclectic variations from extensive wine selections by White House
wine consultant, David Berkeley, to Epicurean European foods and
country-flavored gifts.

✉ 515 Pavillions Lane, Sacramento ☎ 916/929-4422; www.dberkley.com

🕐 Mon–Fri 10–6:30, Sat 10–6, Sun 11–5

Shaker Shops West
Browse the quality reproductions of Shaker furniture and gifts, deep in California's north country.

✉ 5 Inverness Way, Inverness ☎ 415/669-7256; www.shakershops.com
🕐 Fri–Sat 10:30–5

V1870 Marketplace
An excellent enclave of classy shops where you can find gourmet foods, chocolates and wines, as well as fine art.

✉ 6525 Washington Street, Yountville ☎ 707/933-2451; www.vmarketplace.com 🕐 Daily 10:30–5:30

ENTERTAINMENT

Lost Coast Brewery & Café
Microbreweries are the rage, and this is one of the best.

✉ 617 4th Street, Eureka ☎ 707/445-4480; www.lostcoast.com

Old Ironsides
The capital's best venue for live music and dance club nights, with open-mic evenings.

✉ 1901 10th Street, Sacramento ☎ 916/443-9751; www.theoldironsides.com

Paramount Theatre
Sublime art deco building that hosts everything from classical concerts through ballet to rock gigs.

✉ 2025 Broadway, Oakland ☎ 510/465-6400; www.paramounttheatre.com

SPORTS

Ski Lake Tahoe Association
Package deals are available on the 15 downhill and 11 cross-country ski areas, with a free shuttle between all.

☎ 800/588-7668; www.skilaketahoe.com

Yosemite Mountaineering School
Rock-climbing, backpacking, camping and hiking, guided or not. El Capitan mountain attracts climbers in search of a challenge.

☎ 209/372-8344; www.yosemitemountaineering.com

Central Coast

The central coast offers the spectacular Pacific shorelines of Big Sur and the Monterey Peninsula. There are also plenty of parks in which to explore hiking and biking trails. Hearst Castle, which sits high above the shoreline, is an extraordinary architectural link to the California of another era. Morro Bay's beach area is perfect for a slower, more relaxed vacation.

Oxnard

The diversity of the Central Coast is marked by the Danish-influenced town of Solvang. You can see thatched huts and real working windmills and enjoy any number of Scandinavian-style restaurants and shops. Further inland, the Santa Ynez valley boasts several wineries to rival any in the world.

Santa Barbara, Cambria and Montecito are all special in their own way, and should be on the itinerary of any visitor to California.

CARMEL

Carmel was established in the late 19th century and has since gained its reputation as a bohemian retreat. It has some of the most picturesque coastal residences in the state, many in Spanish-Mission style. **Mission San Carlos Borromeo del Rio Carmelo** (1769) was moved to its riverside site here in Carmel in 1771.

✚ 4K

Mission San Carlos Borromeo del Rio Carmelo

✉ 3080 Rio Road ☎ 831/624-1271; www.carmelmission.org 🕐 Mon–Sat 9:30–5, Sun 10:30–5 ✋ Inexpensive

HEARST CASTLE

Best places to see, ➤ 44–45.

MONTEREY PENINSULA

Best places to see, ➤ 48–49.

MORRO BAY

Morro Rock, the conical, volcano-shaped rock that towers 578ft (176m) out of the Pacific Ocean, sits guarding the entrance to Morro Bay, which is known primarily for its commercial fishing and oyster farming. Although the town has a modest tourist trade, the locals are mostly concerned with the daily business of fishing. Beneath the rock stretches a long beach with 85ft-high (26m) white sand dunes that serve as a habitat for bird and plant life.

The Morro Bay Arts Festival takes place each weekend in October, and the **Museum of Natural History** exhibits marine life native to the central coast, including the Bay's entertaining sea lions. **Tiger's Folly Cruises** offers harbor cruises.

The State Park, south of Morro Bay, is beautiful and a must for those who enjoy camping and hiking. The campgrounds are at the southern end of the park surrounded by cypress and eucalyptus.

www.morrobay.org

🚩 5M

ℹ️ Chamber of Commerce, 45 Embarcadero Road, Suite D; tel: 805/772-4467; Mon–Fri 9–5, Sat 10–4, Sun 10–2

Museum of Natural History

✉️ Morro Bay State Park ☎ 805/772-2694; www.morrobaymuseum.org 🕐 Daily 10–5 🎟️ Inexpensive

Tiger's Folly Cruises

✉️ 1205 Embarcadero ☎ 805/772-2257 🕐 Call for times 🎟️ Moderate

OXNARD

Oxnard is a harbor town on the Ventura–Los Angeles county line, and is home to an annual Strawberry Festival each May. Often overlooked by visitors are the beautiful beaches lining the town.

The **Carnegie Art Museum** has a permanent collection of 20th-century California painters, while changing exhibits feature photography and sculpture, with some shows spotlighting local artists. The **Ventura County Gull Wings Children's Museum's** hands-on exhibits of fossils and minerals, including a puppet theater and make-believe campground, will entertain the kids.

🚩 8W

Carnegie Art Museum

✉️ 424 S "C" Street ☎ 805/385-8157; www.carnegieam.org 🕐 Thu–Sat 10–5, Sun 1–5 🎟️ Inexpensive

Ventura County Gull Wings Children's Museum

✉️ 418 W 4th Street ☎ 805/483-3005; www.gullwings.org 🕐 Tue–Fri 10–4, Sat 10–5, Sun noon–4 🎟️ Inexpensive

SALINAS

John Steinbeck was born in this working-class town 17 miles (27km) inland from Monterey, now home to the **National Steinbeck Center.** While it's sometimes overlooked in favor of its more affluent neighbors, Salinas is charming. For those visiting in August, there is the Steinbeck Festival. Many rodeo fans visit the town in July to catch one of the major stops on the professional rodeo circuit.

The Hat In Three Stages of Landing is a unique giant sculpture by Claes Oldenberg, which captures a trio of bright yellow hats, each weighing 3,500lb (1,590kg). The sculpture graces the lawn of the Community Center, where there are art exhibits and musical/theatrical performances.

➕ 4K

National Steinbeck Center

✉ 1 Main Street ☎ 831/796-3833; www.steinbeck.org ⏱ Daily 10–5; closed major hols ✋ Moderate

SANTA BARBARA

A pleasant and affordable day trip from Los Angeles by train (moderate cost) taking you along the Pacific coast in the morning, gives you time to explore the historic adobes and museums. Lunch on Stearns Wharf, explore the specialty shops there, then stroll the white-sand beach, or play a short round of golf before returning in late afternoon.

The County Courthouse, on Anacapa Street, is one of the best examples of Spanish-Moorish architecture in the US.

El Presidio de Santa Barbara State Historic Park, on the site of a late-1700 Spanish outpost, includes historical buildings such as El Cuartel, the second-oldest surviving edifice in California.

Mission Santa Barbara is the best preserved of the 21 California missions, and the church is filled with Mexican art from the 18th and 19th centuries. A Moorish fountain from 1808 graces the front and the mission is the site of The Little Fiesta each August.

The **Santa Barbara Museum of Art** has a variety of American, Asian and 19th-century French, Greek and Roman antiquities, including a photographic collection. Visit the Zoological Gardens, which are natural habitats for 600 animals, with over 80 exhibits.

✚ 8W

El Presidio de Santa Barbara State Historic Park
✉ 122–129 E Canon Perdido Street ☎ 805/965-0093; www.sbthp.org 🕐 Daily 10:30–4:30 ✋ Free

Mission Santa Barbara
✉ E Los Olivos and Laguna Street ☎ 805/682-4149; www.santabarbaramission.org 🕐 Daily 9–5; closed major hols ✋ Inexpensive, under 16 free

Santa Barbara Museum of Art
✉ 1130 State Street ☎ 805/963-4364; www.sbmuseart.org 🕐 Tue–Sun 11–5 ✋ Moderate; free Sun

SOLVANG
Denmark in California might best describe Solvang, with its Danish architecture, windmills, gaslights and cobblestone walks. A tour of Solvang is possible in a horse-drawn Danish streetcar, and the town hosts several remarkable festivals annually. Contrasting the Scandinavian motif is the 1804 **Old Mission Santa Ines.**
www.solvangusa.com

✚ 7V

Old Mission Santa Ines
✉ 1760 Mission Drive ☎ 805/688-4815; www.missionsantaines.org
🕐 Jun–Sep 9–6, Oct–May 9–5:30; closed major hols ✋ Inexpensive
ℹ Conference & Visitors Bureau, 1639 Copenhagen Drive; tel: 805/688-6144

VENTURA

This small beach town between Los Angeles and Santa Barbara is worth a brief visit.

San Buenaventura Mission was founded in 1782 by Father Junípero Serra and was reputed to be his favorite mission. The church is restored and the museum exhibits Native American artifacts from the Chumash tribes.

Next to the Mission is the Albinger Archaeological Museum. It displays over 3,500 years of remains, all from areas around the Mission, while Ventura County Museum of History and Art has Native American, Hispanic and pioneer exhibits.

🔁 8W

San Buenaventura Mission

✉ 211 East Main Street ☎ 805/643-4318; www.sanbuenaventuramission.org
🕐 Mon–Fri 10–5, Sat 9–5, Sun 10–4; closed major hols 👆 Inexpensive

HOTELS

BIG SUR
▼▼▼ Ventana Inn & Spa ($$$)
A luxurious hideaway comprising 59 separate bungalows with sweeping views of the coastline.

✉ 48123 California Highway 1 ☎ 831/667-2331; www.ventanainn.com

CARMEL
▼▼ Carmel River Inn ($)
This place offers a mixture of compact motel-style rooms and more spacious cottages, as well as easy access to the ocean.

✉ 26600 Oliver Road ☎ 831/624-1575; www.carmelriverinn.com

▼▼▼ Sandpiper Inn by the Sea ($$)
An early California inn built in 1929, and some rooms have splendid ocean views.

✉ 2408 Bay View Avenue ☎ 831/624-6433; www.sandpiper-inn.com

MONTEREY
▼▼▼▼ Old Monterey Inn ($$$)
English country hotel boasting acres of gardens and spectacular views of Monterey Bay. The rooms are luxurious and stylish.

✉ 500 Martin Street ☎ 831/375-8284; www.oldmontereyinn.com

SANTA BARBARA
▼▼▼ Hotel Santa Barbara ($$)
The pleasant Mediterranean ambience and downtown location make this a good choice. Well furnished individual rooms.

✉ 533 State Street ☎ 805/957-9300; www.hotelsantabarbara.com

RESTAURANTS

MONTECITO
▼▼▼ Montecito Cafe ($$)
California cuisine; some excellent seafood salads complement the mainly meaty entrées. Warm setting in The Montecito Inn.

✉ 1295 Coast Village Road ☎ 805/969-3392; www.montecinocafe.com
⏰ Daily 11:30–2:30, 5:30–10

MONTEREY
✇✇✇ The C Restaurant ($$$)
Top-quality place with magnificent ocean views and superb dishes such as lobster bisque and roasted California rack of lamb.

✉ 750 Cannery Row ☎ 831/375-4800; www.thecrestaurant-monterey.com
🕐 Daily 6:30–11, 5:30–10

MORRO BAY
✇✇✇ Hoppe's Garden Bistro ($$$)
International cuisine and a great wine list; the vast menu includes smoked pheasant pizza with carmelized onions.

✉ 78 North Ocean Avenue, Cayucos ☎ 805/772-9012 🕐 Wed–Sun 11–10

OJAI
✇✇ Suzanne's Cuisine ($$)
A real gem off the beaten path serving excellent California cuisine. There are fine pasta dishes, as well as a mean bouillabaise.

✉ 502 W Ojai Avenue ☎ 805/ 640-1961; www.suzannescuisine.com
🕐 Wed–Mon 11:30–2:30, 5:30–11

SAN LUIS OBISPO
✇✇✇ Buona Tavola ($$)
A great-value Italian restaurant in a casual, country setting. The veal *scaloppini* with portabello mushrooms is a winner.

✉ 1037 Monterey Street ☎ 805/545-8000; www.btslo.com 🕐 Mon –Fri 11:30–2:30, 5:30–9:30, Sat–Sun 5:30–9:30

SANTA BARBARA
✇✇✇ Boathouse ($$$)
The predominantly seafood menu has influences from the Pacific rim and Latin America, such as the mesquite grilled mahi mahi.

✉ 2981 Cliff Drive, Hendry's Beach ☎ 805/898-2628; www.sbfishhouse.com
🕐 Daily 7am–9:30pm

✇✇ Carlito's Cafe y Cantina ($)
Come here for budget Mexican and interesting vegetarian plates.

✉ 1324 State Street ☎ 805/962-7117; www.carlitos.com 🕐 Daily 11–11

SHOPPING

American Tin Cannery Outlets
Izod and Nine West are just two of the nearly 40 stores.

✉ 125 Ocean View Boulevard, Pacific Grove, Monterey

🖥 www.americantincannery.com

Pismo Beach Prime Outlets
Jones New York, Bass, Mikasa, Levi's; 40 shops in all.

✉ 333 5-Cities Drive, Pismo Beach ☎ www.premiumoutlets.com

Solvang Outlet Stores
Small but élite, featuring Donna Karen, Ellen Tracy, Brooks Bros.

✉ 3202 N Alisal Road, Solvang

ENTERTAINMENT

Center Stage Theater
This modern venue stages musicals, dance performances and various types of theatrical productions.

✉ Paseo Nuevo Center, Chapala Street, Santa Barbara ☎ 805/963-8198; www.centerstagetheater.org

Christopher Cohen Performing Arts Center
Stage plays, opera, ballet, dance and classical music concerts all feature at the town's main cultural venue.

✉ 1 Grand Avenue, San Luis Obispo ☎ 805/756-7222; www.pacslo.org

The Mucky Duck
There's a British influence in the Tudor look and menu at this pub, which has occasional live music, DJ sets and games.

✉ 479 Alvarado Street, Monterey ☎ 831/655-3031; www.muckyduckmonterey.com

Velvet Jones
This lively club hosts different types of shows, from indie rock through reggae to comedy acts.

✉ 423 State Street, Santa Barbara ☎ 805/965-8676; www.velvet-jones.com

Los Angeles

Los Angeles □

Whether you come for the beaches, mountains, museums or movie stars, Los Angeles teems with activity. Bring your sunglasses and your tanning lotion because at this end of California there is plenty of sunshine. For dedicated sun-seekers, beautiful beaches stretch along the western edge of this seemingly endless metropolis. Zuma Beach is one of the best for enjoying the pastime made famous by the music of The Beach Boys – surfing.

At Venice Beach you can either stroll barefoot along the beach or join the hustle along the Boardwalk, where vendors hawk their souvenirs. This is home to some of the nation's most colorful characters: musicians, magicians and mime artists, as well as Muscle Beach body builders.

BEVERLY HILLS

The City of Stars is the place where shopping and the entertainment industry each vie for their place as the number one attraction (➤ 134–135). Here you will find some of the most expensive real estate in the country. The city's most recognizable zip code (90210) receives more than 14 million visitors a year, making it the most popular destination in Los Angeles.

Beverly Hills has several main thoroughfares, all running east to west. Sunset Boulevard, at the north end, roughly splits the commercial and residential areas. Wilshire Boulevard is the main thoroughfare to the business and commercial centers. At the south end, Pico Boulevard marks the Beverly Hills border.

www.beverlyhillsbehere.com

✚ 9W

🛈 239 S Beverly Drive, Beverly Hills 90212; tel: 800/345–2210; Mon–Fri 8:30–5

CHINATOWN

The cultural center of this unique community is home to about five percent of LA's 200,000 Chinese residents. Chinatown encompasses 16 square blocks, and its downtown area is filled with Asian architecture, good restaurants and import shops. The Kong Chow Temple is exquisite.

✚ *Downtown LA 4c* ✉ 900 block of Broadway

CITY HALL

This was the first skyscraper to be built in Los Angeles and served as The Daily Planet Building in the *Superman* television series of the 1950s. Guided

tours are free (weekdays 10am–1pm) and last 45 minutes. There's an observation deck on the 27th floor.

🚩 *Downtown LA 3e* ✉ 200 N Spring Street ☎ 213/978-0721 ⏰ Mon–Fri 9–4 ✋ Free

DESCANSO GARDENS

These glorious gardens cover 65 acres (26ha), including a 30-acre (12ha) California live oak forest. Over 100,000 camellias from around the world flourish here, as do many roses, lilacs and other blossoms. The Japanese Garden has a serene teahouse, worth a visit.

www.descansogardens.org

🚩 10W ✉ 1418 Descanso Drive, La Cañada Flintridge ☎ 818/949-4200 ⏰ Daily 9–5; closed Christmas Day ✋ Inexpensive, special discounts

EL PUEBLO DE LOS ANGELES STATE HISTORICAL MONUMENT

Here, on 44 acres (18ha) near downtown, you can visit the Avila Adobe (the oldest adobe house), Masonic Hall, Old Plaza Church and Sepulveda House. Founded in 1781, the main attraction for most visitors is Olvera Street, an open-air Mexican-style market place lined with specialty shops, vendors, cafés and restaurants.

🚩 *Downtown LA 4d* ✉ Betweeen Alameda, Arcadia, Spring and Macy streets ☎ 213/628-1274 ⏰ Hours vary, call for times ✋ Free

a walk around Beverly Hills

This walk begins on one of the most exclusive and expensive shopping streets in the world.

Walk north from Wilshire on Rodeo Drive.

Do a spot of window-shopping in Tiffany's, Saks and other high-end boutiques.

Proceed north several blocks to Little Santa Monica, then go east (right) a couple of blocks to Crescent.

On the corner of Crescent you'll see the historic former Beverly Hills Post Office and the magnificent Beverly Hills Municipal Building. The latter houses City Hall and the Beverly Hills library and police station.

Take a left on Crescent and proceed north across Santa Monica Boulevard and through the Beverly Hills "flatlands."

The homes along here are absolutely gorgeous.

At Sunset Boulevard, walk across to the restored Beverly Hills Hotel (▶ 144).

Take a few minutes to stroll through the splendid lobby.

Proceed east on Sunset to the West Hollywood business district.

Here you will pass the famous Roxy theater, Spago restaurant and The Whiskey A Go-Go.

Continue east, stopping for lunch at Restaurant Clafoutis. Turn right on Crescent Heights Road and go south to Melrose Avenue. Turn left on to Melrose and walk several blocks to Fairfax Avenue.

At this corner is the sprawling CBS Television City. Here you can get free tickets to live tapings of television shows.

South of CBS is the Farmers Market and the Grove, where your tour comes to an end.

Distance 7 miles (6.5km)
Time 5 hours, depending on time spent at attractions
Start point Beverly Hills, corner of Wilshire and Rodeo
End point Farmers Market and the Grove complex of shops, restaurants and movie theaters
Lunch Restaurant Clafoutis ($$), 8630 Sunset Boulevard; tel: 310/659-5233

EXPOSITION PARK

The Los Angeles Memorial Coliseum was host to the Olympics in 1932 and 1984. Several museums are contained within, including the **California Museum of Science and Industry,** with interactive exhibits, Aerospace Complex and the surround-vision IMAX theater, featuring a five-story-high screen. Other museums include the **California Afro-American Museum** and the **Los Angeles County Museum of Natural History,** with three floors of dinosaur, fossil and cultural exhibits.

✚ Downtown LA 1e (off map)

California Museum of Science and Industry

✉ Exposition Boulevard at Figueroa ☎ 213/744-7400; www.californiasciencecenter.org 🕐 Daily 10–5 ✋ Free, charge for IMAX

California Afro-American Museum

✉ 600 State Drive, Exposition Park ☎ 213/744-7432; www.caamuseum.org 🕐 Tue–Sat 10–5, Sun 11–5 ✋ Free ($8 parking fee)

LA County Museum of Natural History

✉ 900 Exposition Boulevard, Exposition Park ☎ 213/763-3466; www.nhm.org 🕐 Daily 9:30–5 ✋ Moderate; free 1st Tue of month

FOREST LAWN MEMORIAL PARK

There are 300 lush acres (121ha) of grounds here, with reproductions of such works as da Vinci's *Last Supper*, and the world's largest religious painting on canvas, Jan Styke's *The Crucifixion*. Also not to be missed are the ornate tombstones of celebrities and the beautiful gardens. Forest Lawn cemetery is the final resting place of such Hollywood film legends as Humphrey Bogart, Errol Flynn, Spencer Tracy, Stan Laurel, Jean Harlow,

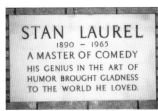

STAN LAUREL
1890 – 1965
A MASTER OF COMEDY
HIS GENIUS IN THE ART OF
HUMOR BROUGHT GLADNESS
TO THE WORLD HE LOVED.

Carole Lombard, W C Fields and Cary Grant.
www.forestlawn.com
➕ 9W ✉ 1712 South Glendale Avenue, Glendale ☎ 800/204-3131 🕐 Daily 8–5 💲 Free

GETTY CENTER

This billion-dollar arts complex sits high on a hill off the 405 San Diego freeway to the north of the city and has become a firm favorite with visitors. With everything from Greek sculptures to paintings by European masters and modern photography, the museum is surrounded by ponds, beautiful landscaping and a fine herb garden.
www.getty.edu
➕ 9W ✉ 1200 Getty Center Drive ☎ 310/440-7300 🕐 Tue–Fri 10–5:30, Sat 10–9, Sun 10–5:30 💲 Free ($15 fee for parking)

GRIFFITH PARK

Here, in the Santa Monica Mountain range, Griffith Park contains the LA Zoo, Griffith Observatory and Planetarium, as well as Travel Town, an outdoor transportation museum. The Observatory is the perfect spot to view the Hollywood sign and the entire city, while the Planetarium features incredible laserium shows. There are horseback riding and children's attractions, plus picnic areas.

🚇 9W ✉ Mount Hollywood ☎ 213/473-0800 (Observatory/Planetarium); 323/644-4200 (Zoo); 323/913-4688 (tourist information) 🕐 Hours vary so call for information 🖐 The park is free; some attractions have moderate fees

HOLLYWOOD

Best places to see, pages 46–47.

HOLLYWOOD WAX MUSEUM

Over 220 of Hollywood's greatest stars, political leaders and sports greats – all made of wax – are on show here. Also included are displays on television, motion pictures and religion. Exhibits rotate every six months or so. The Chamber of Horrors is a favorite, as well as the recent additions of current stars.

www.hollywoodwaxmuseum.com

🚇 9W (Hollywood) ✉ 6767 Hollywood Boulevard ☎ 323/462-5991 🕐 Daily 10–midnight 🖐 Moderate

HUNTINGTON LIBRARY, ART GALLERY AND GARDENS

The historical library contains over four million items, including art treasures and an extraordinary treasury of rare and precious manuscripts. After taking in the Huntington's art and books, take a walk through the immaculate botanical gardens, the best in the

state. Here, 15 separate garden areas contain around 14,000 different types of plants and trees. Arrive early because the grounds fill up fast.
www.huntington.org

✚ 10W ✉ 1151 Oxford Road, San Marino ☎ 626/405-2100 ⏱ Mon, Wed–Fri noon–4:30, Sat–Sun 10:30–4:30 🖐 Moderate

LITTLE TOKYO
The city's Japanese quarter features the 40-shop Japanese Village Plaza, which resembles a rural village. Also here are Noguchi Plaza, with its fan-shaped Japan America Theater, the Japanese American National Museum, and quiet Japanese gardens. Some great sushi bars, too.

✚ Downtown LA 3f ✉ 1st Street and Central Avenue

LONG BEACH

Long Beach is now California's fifth largest city. Its Shoreline Village and Wilmore Park surround the Convention and Entertainment Center. Boats to Catalina Island depart from Golden Shore Boulevard. Of special interest is the *Queen Mary*, which came to rest in Long Beach in 1967. With 12 decks and weighing in at 50,000 tons, it is the largest passenger ship ever built.

➕ 10X

Queen Mary

✉ Pier J, Long Beach Harbor ☎ 562/435-3511 🕐 Daily 10–6 ✋ Expensive

LOS ANGELES COUNTY ARBORETUM

The trees and shrubs in the Los Angeles Arboretum are arranged according to the continent they originate from. Also featured are greenhouses, a bird sanctuary and historic buildings like the Queen Anne Cottage, home of the estate's former owner, Elia Jackson Baldwin. Picnic areas and tours available.

www.arboretum.org

➕ 10W ✉ 301 N Baldwin Avenue, Arcadia ☎ 626/821-3222 🕐 Daily 9–4:30 ✋ Inexpensive; various discounts

MANN'S CHINESE THEATRE

Originally Grauman's Chinese Theatre, Mann's, a prime Hollywood tourist attraction, is a good starting point for a tour of Los Angeles.

The theater was opened in 1927 by showman Sid Grauman, and whenever a film was premiered here, stars left their hand- or footprints.

www.manntheatres.com

9W (Hollywood) 6925 Hollywood Boulevard 323/464-8111

MUSEUM OF CONTEMPORARY ART (MOCA)

This seven-tiered museum (much of it below street level) has 11 giant pyramidal skylights and a 53ft (16m) barrel-vaulted entrance. It is dedicated to works of art since the 1940s and features traveling exhibitions.

www.moca.org

Downtown LA 2e 250 S Grand Avenue 213/621-2766 Mon, Fri 11–5, Thu 11–8, Sat–Sun 11–6 Moderate; free Thu 5–8

PETERSEN AUTOMOTIVE MUSEUM

One of the largest auto collections in the world, which explores automotive history and culture from the earliest jalopies. Highlights are the 1957 Ferrari 250 Testa Rossa, and customized cars from Dean Jeffries and George Barris. A must for automotive fans.

www.petersen.org

Downtown LA 1c (off map) 6060 Wilshire Boulevard 323/930-2277 Tue–Sun 10–6 Moderate

SANTA MONICA

At the centre of the 20 mile (32km) stretch of beach that lines the eponymous bay, Santa Monica may not be quite as trendy as Malibu or Venice but it offers a greater variety of shopping, dining and accommodations. It also has an impressive pier and the great **Museum of Art**.

✚ 9W

Museum of Art

✉ 2525 Michigan Avenue ☎ 310/586-6488; www.smmoa.org 🕐 Tue–Sat 11–6

UNIVERSAL STUDIOS AND CITYWALK

For a fascinating behind-the-scenes look at movie-making, plan to spend the better part of a day at Universal Studios, the world's biggest and busiest motion picture and television studio-cum-theme park. Citywalk features outdoor dining and a wide variety of shops that are a cut above what you might expect. There are huge outdoor screens that show music videos and movie previews and a theater complex shows all the latest movies.

The upper and lower sections are connected by a long escalator, making the 420-acre (170ha) park easy to navigate. Some of the classic movie-related attractions and rides to be enjoyed are the Bates Motel, Jaws, the War of the Worlds and the new King Kong 360 3-D display, created by Peter Jackson.

www.universalstudioshollywood.com

✈ 9W (Hollywood) ✉ 100 Universal City Plaza, Universal City ☎ 800/864-8377 🕐 Daily from 9 or 10am; closing hours vary ✋ Expensive

VENICE BEACH

Just south along the beach from Santa Monica is Venice Beach. Although it appears to be a throwback to the 1960s, it is really a thriving enclave for modern bohemians. The neighborhood was founded in 1905 by Abbot Kinney, who hoped to create a haven for artistic types. Gondolas were imported from Italy and, for a time, the canals were eerily similar to those in Europe. Try a free self-guided tour. The most popular today is the Ocean Front Walk, teeming with visitors, street performers and souvenir stands. You can also rent a bicycle or rollerblades.

www.venicebeach.com

✈ 9W ✉ 15 miles (24km) from downtown Los Angeles, access via Lincoln Boulevard

WATTS TOWERS AND ARTS CENTER

Italian immigrant Simon Rodia took 30 years to build these extraordinary towers by himself, using scraps of whatever materials he could find. The Arts Center, next to the towers, contains rotating exhibits of African American art.

www.wattstowers.us

✈ 9W ✉ 1761–65 E 107th Street ☎ 213/473-8343 🕐 Wed–Sat 10–4, Sun noon–4. Tower tours Thu–Sun 10–3 ✋ Inexpensive

HOTELS

The Ambrose ($$)

In a residential neighborhood five minutes by car from the beach, this luxurious boutique hotel offers delightfully decorated rooms.

1225 20th Street, Santa Monica 310/315-1555; www.ambrosehotel.com

Avia Long Beach ($$)

Snazzy new hotel that combines the best of the area's beachside and nightlife activities. Contemporary rooms with all mod cons.

285 Bay Street, Long Beach 562/436-1047; www.aviahotels.com

The Beverly Hills Hotel ($$$)

A 1912 landmark restored in the early 1990s by its owner, the Sultan of Brunei. Famous for its private bungalows and the celebrity-packed Polo Lounge.

9641 Sunset Boulevard 310/276-2251; www.beverlyhillshotel.com

Kyoto Grand Hotel & Gardens ($$)

Japanese-style hotel in the Little Tokyo area of downtown LA. Beautiful gardens and well-appointed rooms.

120 S Los Angeles Street 213/629-1200; www.kyotograndhotel.com

Malibu Beach Inn ($$$)

Mediterranean-style hotel on a white-sand shore. Casual chic is the order of the day from the lobby to the relaxing rooms.

22878 Pacific Coast Highway, Malibu 310/456-6444; www.malibubeachinn.com

Montage Beverly Hills ($$$)

Top-class hotel with lavishly furnished rooms, excellent service and rooftop pool, as well as lovely gardens, shops and two restaurants.

225 N Canon Drive, Beverly Hills 310/860-7800; www.montagebeverlyhills.com

Rodeway Inn & Suites ($)

A standard modern chain hotel located in a quiet suburb, with bright simple rooms and facilities such as a swimming pool and fitness center. Breakfast is included in the price – great value.

✉ 2860 E Colorado Boulevard, Pasadena ☎ 626/792-3700; www.rodewayinn.com

ᐁᐁᐁ Sheraton Universal ($$$)

Views of Hollywood Hills and San Fernando Valley and close to Universal City attractions. Good-value weekend packages.

✉ 333 Universal Hollywood Drive Parkway ☎ 818/980-1212; www.sheratonuniversal.com

ᐁᐁᐁ Sky Hotel ($$)

Pleasant little boutique hotel that shows a great eye for detail in the sleek design. Near the West Side shops and restaurants.

✉ 2352 Westwood Boulevard ☎ 310/475-4551; www.skyhotella.com

ᐁᐁᐁ ᐁᐁᐁ Sofitel Los Angeles ($$)

Mediterranean-style hotel with extremely comfortable and spacious rooms. Across from the Beverly Center mall (➤ 150).

✉ 8555 Beverly Boulevard ☎ 310/278-5444; www.sofitella.com

ᐁᐁᐁ ᐁᐁᐁ Sunset Marquis ($$$)

Mostly suites, this hotel is a favorite of the entertainment community for its casual atmosphere and Mediterranean decor.

✉ 1200 N Alta Loma Road ☎ 310/657-1333; www.sunsetmarquis.com

ᐁᐁ Super 8 North Hollywood ($)

This branch of the trusty motel chain is one of the best budget options within easy reach of the glitz and glamour of Hollywood.

✉ 7541 Laurel Canyon Road, North Hollywood ☎ 818/765-9800; www.super8.com

RESTAURANTS

ᵂᵂ Dan Tana's ($$$)

Long-time celebrity hangout for Italian food; the best steaks and fresh lobster. Very Hollywood.

✉ 9071 Santa Monica Boulevard ☎ 310/275-9444; www.dantanasrestaurant.com 🕐 Daily 5–1:30

ᵂᵂ El Cholo Café ($$)

Long-established family-owned Mexican serving traditional fare since 1927. The original of five LA locations.

✉ 1121 S Western Avenue ☎ 323/734-2773; www.elcholo.com 🕐 Mon–Thu 11–10, Fri–Sat 11–11, Sun 11–9

ᵂᵂ Gin Sushi ($$)

You can enjoy a wide selection of extremely fresh sushi and other favorite Japanese dishes in this bright modern restaurant.

✉ 3589 E Colorado Boulevard, Pasadena ☎ 626/440-9611; www.ginsushi.com 🕐 Sun–Thu 11:30–10, Fri–Sat 11:30–10:30

ᵂᵂᵂ Green Field Churrascaria ($$)

After a hard day's surfing you might have room for the huge quantities of meat carved at your table at this Brazilian buffet restaurant.

✉ 5305 E Pacific Coast Highway, Long Beach ☎ 562/597-0906; www.greenfieldchurrascaria.com 🕐 Daily 11–10

ᵂᵂᵂ The Ivy ($$$)

Great American food and the place to see and be seen in LA. Outdoor patio. Reservations are a must.

✉ 113 N Robertson Boulevard ☎ 310/274-8303; www.theivyla.com 🕐 Mon–Thu 11:30–10:30, Fri 11:30–11, Sat 11–11, Sun 10:30–10

ᵂᵂᵂ James' Beach ($$)

A blend of California and Mediterranean cuisines feature on the menu at this trendy beachside place that also serves mean cocktails.

✉ 60 N Venice Boulevard, Venice ☎ 310/823-5396; www.jamesbeach.com 🕐 Wed–Sun 11–3, 6–10:30, Mon–Tue 6–10:30

☜☜☜ Lawry's The Prime Rib ($$$)

The best for prime rib anywhere, supposedly, in the world. "To die for," says one. You decide, but make reservations early.

✉ 100 N La Cienega, Beverley Hills ☎ 866/223-8224;
www.lawrysonline.com 🕐 Mon–Fri 5–10, Sat 4:30–11, Sun 4–9:30

☜☜☜ Matsuhisa ($$$)

The flagship restaurant of the Nobu empire, Matsuhisa serves fantastic sushi and sashimi in a bustling, though slightly cramped, setting. Attracts a trendy crowd.

✉ 129 N La Cienega, Beverly Hills ☎ 310/659-9639;
www.nobumatsuhisa.com 🕐 Mon–Fri 11:45–2:15, 5:45–10:15, Sat–Sun 5:45–10:15

☜☜ Matteo's ($$$)

A one-time Rat Pack hang-out, with roomy leather booths and crimson walls, Matteo's still serves traditional Italian food.

✉ 2321 Westwood Boulevard ☎ 310/475-4521; www.matteosla.com
🕐 Tue–Sat 5:30–10, Sun 5–9

☜☜ Musso & Frank Grill ($$)

A touch of "Old Hollywood" serving traditional fare. Great martinis and the best Caesar salad in LA.

✉ 6667 Hollywood Boulevard ☎ 323/467-7788;
www.mussoandfrankgrill.com 🕐 Tue–Sun noon–10

☜☜ The Original Pantry ($)

Often buzzing even in the wee hours, this 24-hour downtown diner serves up copious quantities of breakfasts, burgers and steaks.

✉ 877 S Figueroa Street ☎ 213/972-9279; www.pantrycafe.com
🕐 Daily 24 hours

☜☜☜ Pacific Dining Car ($$$)

Downtown standard for steaks and seafood, this restaurant is most atmospheric in the evening, when reservations are essential.

✉ 1310 W 6th Street ☎ 213/483-6000; www.pacificdiningcar.com
🕐 Daily 24 hours.

▽▽▽ Parkway Grill ($$)

The multi-ethnic cuisine is worth the trip to Pasadena, but there's also California fare. Try the Thai tiger shrimp corndogs.

✉ 510 S Arroyo Parkway, Pasadena ☎ 626/795-1001; www.theparkwaygrill.com ⏰ Mon–Fri 11:30–2:30, 5:30–9:30, Sat–Sun 5:30–9:30

▽▽▽ ▽▽▽ Patina ($$$)

Comfortable and unpretentious French bistro where you can splurge on the $130 tasting menu.

✉ 141 S Grand Avenue ☎ 213/972-3331; www.patinarestaurant.com ⏰ Tue–Sat 5–9:30, Sun 4–9

▽▽▽ Prado Restaurant ($$)

Wonderful dishes from around the Americas and Carribean are featured at this friendly place. Try the shrimp in Jamaican black pepper sauce.

✉ 244 N Larchmont Boulevard ☎ 323/467-3871; www.pradola.com ⏰ Mon–Fri 11:30–3, 5:30–10, Sat 11:30–3, 4:30–10:30, Sun 4:30–9:30

▽▽▽ ▽▽▽ Spago ($$$)

World-renowned for chef Wolfgang Puck's gourmet pizzas, and its star-studded Academy Awards party. Also fine California cuisine.

✉ 176 N Canon Drive, Beverly Hills ☎ 310/385-0880; www.wolfgangpuck.com ⏰ Lunch Mon–Sat, dinner daily; hours vary

▽▽ Tibet Nepal House ($)

Plenty of traditional treats from the Himalayas, such as *momos* and *daal bhaat*, are available at this great-value restaurant.

✉ 36 E Holly Street, Pasadena ☎ 626/585-0955; www.tibetnepalhouse.com ⏰ Daily 11:30–2:30, 5–10

▽▽▽ ▽▽▽ Valentino ($$$)

Elegant, expensive Italian with a great wine list and impeccable service. Reservations required.

✉ 3115 Pico Boulevard, Santa Monica ☎ 310/829-4313; www.valentinorestaurantgroup.com ⏰ Tue–Thu 5–10, Fri 11:30–2:30, 5–10:30, Sat 5–10:30

✈️✈️ Yang Chow ($$)

Somewhat upmarket Chinatown restaurant specializing in Mandarin and Szechuan cuisine, with other branches in Pasadena and Canoga Park.

✉️ 819 N Broadway ☎️ 213/625-0811; www.yangchow.com 🕐 Sun–Thu 11:30–9:45, Fri–Sat 11:30–10:45

SHOPPING

ART AND ANTIQUES

La Cienega Boulevard south of Santa Monica Boulevard, Beverly Boulevard west of the Beverly Center, Melrose Avenue in Hollywood, and Santa Monica's 3rd Street Promenade are all lined with excellent, but costly antiques stores and art galleries.

CRAFTS
Olvera Street

Mexican crafts and gifts, clothing and cafés on LA's oldest street.

✉️ Olvera Street ☎️ www.olvera-street.com

FASHION
Fashion District

Fashion bargains can be found in open store fronts and inside the huge Cooper Building.

✉️ Downtown, 100 blocks centered around E 9th Street

☎️ www.fashiondistrict.org

Melrose Avenue and Rodeo Drive

See page 62.

Venice Beach

See page 143.

GIFTS
Hollywood Boulevard

The place to go to find rare movie memorabilia and posters. Theaters and restaurants for every mood and budget.

✉️ Between La Brea and Highland

Little Tokyo
Unusual Oriental items are sold here, plus outdoor shopping and dining.

✉ San Pedro and 1st streets, Downtown ☎ www.visitlittletokyo.com

Venice Beach
See page 143.

FARMERS MARKET
Over 100 sellers of not only fresh produce but gifts, food and clothes, all at affordable prices. Open-air cafés.

✉ 3rd and Fairfax, Hollywood ☎ www.farmersmarketla.com

STORES
Beverly Center
Three-tiered upscale mall, with exterior elevators that offer a great view of the area; Macy's, Broadway, Bullocks and Hard Rock Café.

✉ Beverly Boulevard and La Cienega, Beverly Hills
☎ www.beverlycenter.com

Westside Pavilion
A multi-level complex with a modern, open-air atrium; Nordstrom, Robinsons-May and others.

✉ Pico and Westwood boulevards ☎ www.westsidepavilion.com

ENTERTAINMENT

NIGHTLIFE
Bar Marmont
This small French colonial café is usually packed with celebrities and paparazzi.

✉ 8171 Sunset Boulevard, Hollywood ☎ 323/650-0575;
www.chateaumarmont.com

BB King's Blues Club
Over three floors. Lucille's room is acoustic on Friday and Saturday.

✉ 1000 Universal City Drive, Universal City ☎ 818/622-5464;
www.bbkingclubs.com

Cat & Fiddle Pub and Restaurant
Ambient outdoor patio and British pub touches inside. Sunday jazz jam. No cover.
✉ 6530 Sunset Boulevard, Hollywood ☎ 323/468-3800;
www.thecatandfiddle.com

Cowboy Palace Saloon
The last real honky tonk in California with live country seven nights a week. Pool, darts and dance classes. No cover.
✉ 21635 Devonshire Street, Chatsworth ☎ 818/341-0166;
www.cowboypalace.com

Good Luck Bar
Knocked out of the No 1 spot by Bar Marmont, but now you finally have room to dance and enjoy yourself.
✉ 1514 Hillhurst Avenue, Los Feliz ☎ 323/666-3524

The Improvisation (Improv)
See the place where many comedians, such as Richard Pryer, Eddie Murphy and Jay Leno, got their start.
✉ 8162 Melrose, West Hollywood ☎ 323/651-2583; www.theimprov.com

The Mint
Enjoy top-class live jazz, blues and R&B in this small club.
✉ 6010 Pico Boulevard ☎ 323/954-9400; www.themintla.com

Molly Malone's Irish Pub
Small neighborhood bar with Irish folk, rock & roll, R&B nightly.
✉ 575 S Fairfax ☎ 323/935-1577; www.mollymaleonesla.com

Rage
Gay and lesbian meeting place, playing mostly house music.
✉ 8911 Santa Monica Boulevard, West Hollywood ☎ 310/652-7055

PERFORMING ARTS
Hollywood Bowl
Outdoor arena with year-round headline concerts of every music

151

style, especially the LA Philharmonic.

✉ 2301 N Highland Avenue, Hollywood ☎ 323/850-2000;
www.hollywoodbowl.com

Music Center of Los Angeles County

Includes Dorothy Chandler Pavilion and Mark Taper Forum featuring
experiment plays, and the Ahmanson with musical comedies and
the Walt Disney Concert Hall.

✉ 135 N Grand, Downtown ☎ 213/972-7211; www.musiccenter.org

Wiltern Theatre

Intimate, acoustically wonderful hall that features top-name
musical performances in the art deco Wiltern Center.

✉ 3790 Wiltshire Boulevard ☎ 213/480-3232

SPORTS

Los Angeles Dodgers

LA's legendary basefall team play at Dodger Stadium.

✉ 1000 Elysian Park Avenue ☎ 323/224-1507; www.losangelesdodgers.mlb.com

Los Angeles Galaxy

The Los Angeles soccer team play at the Home Depot Center.

✉ 18400 Avalon Boulevard, Carson ☎ 310/630-2200; www.lagalaxy.com

Moonlight Rollerway

Moonlight is one of the more popular indoor roller-blading rinks.

✉ 5110 San Fernando Road, Glendale ☎ 818/241-3630;
www.moonlightrollerway.com

Pershing Square

The outdoor ice rink in Pershing Square opens in November.

✉ Pershing Square Station on Metro Red Line ☎ 818/243-6488

Santa Anita Race Track

Bet on horses during the track's season, from December to April.

✉ 285 West Huntington Drive ☎ 626/574-7223 ◷ Dec 26–late Apr;
www.santaanita.com

Southern California

The commercial center of the state, Southern California is the most densley populated area. The vast metropolitan areas of Los Angeles and San Diego are surrounded by largely empty deserts.

San Diego

Southern California is also the center of the entertainment and aerospace industries. Hollywood, Disneyland and the many beaches that stretch south to Mexico are the favorites of most people who visit the area. There is a distinct Spanish influence in the architecture, and most of the missions are located along the coast between San Diego and Los Angeles.

BAKERSFIELD

Bakersfield is California's main oil-producing center. Many consider it a less-than-desirable part of California, its furnace-like, 100°F-plus (38°C) summers a major drawback. However, the downtown area is a mix of restored buildings and newer offices. Of note are a genuine schoolhouse, church and a fully restored 1868 log cabin.

The **California Living Museum** focuses on the state's wildlife and native plants, many of which are rare or endangered.

Kern County Museum has exhibits representing both the human and the natural history of the area.

✠ 9U

California Living Museum

✉ 10500 Alfred Harrell Highway ☎ 661/872-2256; www.calmzoo.org
🕐 Daily 9–5 (Oct–Feb until 4) 🍴 Picnic facilities ✋ Inexpensive

Kern County Museum

✉ 3801 Chester Avenue ☎ 661/852-5000; www.kcmuseum.org
🕐 Wed–Sun 10–5 ✋ Moderate

BARSTOW

Barstow stands at the halfway point between Los Angeles and Las Vegas. It was settled in the early 19th century when silver mines flourished in the surrounding areas. The town of **Calico** boomed in the late 1800s, and its mines produced $15 million worth of ore. When the price of silver dropped, the town went bust. Today, you can visit the "ghost town" of Calico to pan for gold, ride the steam railway or see a show at the Calikage Playhouse.

North of Barstow is **Rainbow Basin National Natural Landmark.** Fossils, the forces of nature and an abundance of minerals give it its dramatic shapes and colors.

🚹 11V

Calico Ghost Town

✉ 11 miles (18km) northeast of Barstow via I-15 ☎ 760/254-2122; www.calicotown.com 🕐 Daily 9–5 🍴 Restaurants ($$) 💵 Inexpensive

Rainbow Basin National Natural Landmark

✉ Fossil Bed Road, 8 miles (13km) north of Barstow via SR 58

BIG BEAR LAKE

One of California's largest recreation areas, the Big Bear Lake region has two distinct sections; Big Bear Lake and Big Bear City, on the eastern end of the lake. Big Bear Village, centered around the lake, is popular for lodging, dining and shopping. Camping, hiking and riding are available in summer and skiing in winter.

www.bigbearchamber.com

🚹 11W 🍴 Many restaurants ($–$$$)

ℹ Big Bear Chamber of Commerce, 630 Bartlett Road; tel: 909/866-4607

CATALINA ISLAND

Best places to see, ▶ 38–39.

DEATH VALLEY NATIONAL PARK

Three million years ago, forces within the earth tormented, twisted and shook the land in what is now Death Valley, creating snowcapped mountains and superheated valleys. Lakes, formed during the Ice Age, evaporated, leaving alternating layers of mud and salt deposits.

More than three million acres in size, Death Valley ranges in elevation from 282ft (86m) below sea level to slightly over 11,000 (3,354m) above. Temperatures reach well over 120°F in summer, making it one of the hottest regions in the world.

Scotty's Castle, on the northern boundary of the park, is a Spanish/Moorish construction built by Chicago insurance tycoon Albert Johnson for Walter E. Scott, alias "Death Valley Scotty."

🔢 11S ✉ Furnace Creek Visitors Center ☎ 760/786-3244 🕐 Daily 8–5 ✋ Moderate ❓ Camping facilities

Scotty's Castle

☎ 760/786-2392 🕐 Daily 8–5 ✋ Moderate

FRESNO

Fresno lies in the heart of the San Joaquin Valley. One of the foremost agricultural areas in the country, it is also the gateway to the Sierra Nevada's three national parks.

The **Fresno Art Museum** contains an impressive permanent collection and rotating exhibitions of mostly contemporary art. Wild Water Adventure Park, on E Shaw Avenue, contains over 20 water rides, pools and a small fishing lake.

➕ 8S

Fresno Art Museum

✉ 2233 N 1st Street ☎ 559/441-4221 ◷ Tue–Sun 11–5
✋ Inexpensive; Sun free

JOSHUA TREE NATIONAL PARK

Known for its distinctive Joshua trees (a desert tree of the yucca species), and its unique rock formations, the park connects the "high" and "low" deserts. Inside is Key's View, a high elevation with incredible views on a clear day. Don't miss the Cholla Cactus Garden, 10 miles (16km) south of the Oasis Visitors Center.
www.nps.gov/jotr

✚ 12X ✉ Oasis Vistors Center, National Monument Drive, 29 Palms ☎ 760/367-5500 ◷ Visitor Center daily 8–5; park always open ✋ Inexpensive

LAKE ARROWHEAD

Known locally as a sophisticated mountain getaway, Lake Arrowhead is where LA's wealthy spend leisurely weekends in luxury homes. Fortunately, restrictive development laws help preserve the area's natural beauty. Swimming and boating are the most popular activities in summer, and skiing in winter. Children will enjoy the **Lake Arrowhead Children's Museum,** with historical information on the area and anthropological exhibitions.
www.lakearrowhead.net

✚ 11W 🛈 Chamber of Commerce, Lake Arrowhead Village; tel: 909/337-3715; Mon–Fri 9–5, Sat 10–3

Lake Arrowhead Children's Museum

✉ Lake Arrowhead Village ☎ 909/336-3093 🕐 Daily 10–5, 10–6 in summer 🖐 Inexpensive

ORANGE COUNTY

Known by Californians as the "conservative" enclave of the state, Orange County is a sprawling expanse of humanity between Los Angeles and San Diego, with its own unique charms.

Anaheim

Anaheim was founded as the center of a wine-producing colony by German immigrants in 1857. The vineyards were replaced by orange groves late in the 19th century, after a brutal drought. Oranges thrived until the 1950s, when commercial interests and the rapid growth of the Los Angeles metropolitan area took over. The two main attractions in the area are **Disneyland Park** (Best places to see ➤ 40–41) and Knott's Berry Farm (➤ 160).

➕ 10X ✉ 46 miles (74km) from Los Angeles via I–5

Festival of the Arts/Pageant of the Masters

A state-of-the-art art exhibit in the scenic wooded Laguna Canyon, this is a landmark event, the former featuring an exhibit of 150 Laguna artists of all kinds. The most interesting aspect of this seven-week event, however, is the Pageant of the Masters, in which human models stand perfectly still for three minutes as re-creations of famous paintings and sculptures, with a suitable musical accompaniment.

www.foapom.com

➕ 10X ✉ Laguna Canyon Road, Laguna Beach ☎ 949/494-1145

🕐 Jul–Aug 10am–11pm ✋ Expensive

Huntington Beach Art Center

Though small, the Huntington Art Center is concerned with local contemporary art and architecture in a big way. It has been renovated and is a favorite with many local artists. Films are shown the first and third Friday of each month.

➕ 10X ✉ 538 Main Street E, Huntington Beach ☎ 714/374-1650

🕐 Wed–Sat noon–6 ✋ Free

International Surfing Museum

Huntington Beach calls itself "Surf City" and is a mecca for surfing enthusiasts. Exhibits tell the sport's history, and the store sells surf gear, all, of course, to the music of the Beach Boys.

➕ 10X ✉ 411 Olive Avenue, Huntington Beach ☎ 714/960-3483; www.surfingmuseum.org 🕐 Mon, Wed–Fri 12–5, Tue noon–9, Sat–Sun 11–6

✋ Inexpensive

Knott's Berry Farm

One of California's original theme parks, Knott's has grown from a berry farm to a modern 150-acre (61ha) attraction with over 165 rides. The Western theme areas include Ghost Town and Indian Trails. Other attractions include Camp Snoopy, Wild Water Wilderness, Mystery Lodge, Reflection Lake, Knott's Marketplace and Kingdom of the Dinosaurs. There are some truly enervating rides, including La Revolucion, Rip Tide and Supreme Scream. For the truly hungry, Knott's serves its world-famous boysenberry pie.

www.knotts.com

🕂 10X 📧 8039 Beach Boulevard, Buena Park ☎ 714/220-5200 🕔 Hours vary; call for current times 💷 Expensive

Laguna Art Museum

The Laguna Art Museum was founded in 1918 and is the showcase venue for the Laguna Art Association. It usually features several visiting exhibits of paintings and sculpture by California artists. On permanent display are historical California landscapes and vintage photographs of the region.

www.laguanaartmuseum.org

🕂 10X 📧 Pacific Coast Highway and Cliff Drive, Laguna Beach ☎ 949/494-8971 🕔 Daily 11–5 💷 Inexpensive

Mission San Juan Capistrano

Founded in 1776, this is one of California's most beautiful missions, and the only building still standing where Father Junípero Serra said Mass. On 19 March each year, the Feast of St. Joseph celebrates the legendary "return of the swallows."

🕂 10X 📧 Corner of Ortega Highway/Camino Capistrano ☎ 949/234-1300 🕔 Daily 8:30–5 💷 Inexpensive

Santa Ana

A typical thriving small city in Orange County, Santa Ana centers around the South Coast Plaza, a European-styled mall with shops,

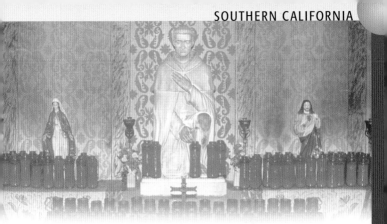

restaurants and cinemas. The **Bowers Museum of Cultural Art,** a mission-style museum, is the largest in Orange County. It focuses on American, Pacific and African art, with an impressive permanent collection and quarterly visiting exhibits.

✚ 10X

Bowers Museum of Cultural Art

✉ 2002 N Main Street ☎ 714/567-3600; www.bowers.org 🕐 Tue–Sun 10–4 ✋ Moderate

Sherman Library and Gardens

The unique gardens are filled with orchids and koi ponds, while the library itself takes up a whole city block. It functions as a center of historical research for the region. There is an extensive collection of historical Orange County documents and photographs.

www.slgardens.org

✚ 10X ✉ 2647 E Coast Highway, Newport Beach ☎ 949/673-2261 🕐 Gardens daily 10:30–4 ✋ Inexpensive

Yorba Linda

The **Richard Nixon Presidential Library and Birthplace**, in Yorba Linda, has galleries, theaters and gardens, and personal memorabilia of this former US president. The grounds feature the house where he was born and his post-presidency private study.

✚ 10X ✉ 18001 Yorba Linda Boulevard ☎ 714/993-3393 🕐 Mon–Sat 10–5, Sun 11–5 ✋ Inexpensive

PALM SPRINGS

Rising out of the desert like an oasis, Palm Springs is one of the most famous resort towns in the world. It has become a favorite of wealthy retirees with a penchant for good golf and bad driving habits, and an ever-increasing number of young people are looking here for a brief spring retreat from their studies. The summers are insufferably hot, however, and the population dwindles from June through early September.

Anza-Borrego Desert State Park offers spectacular desert scenery. Set in 600,000 acres (242,915ha), the main flora includes lupin, poppy, dune primrose, desert sunflower and desert lily. A variety of short trails and campgrounds can be found here.

Five miles (8km) south of Palm Springs is **Agua Caliente Indian Reservation.** The Tribal Council here has opened part of the reservation for hiking and picnics.

An awesome view of the San Jacinto Mountains awaits if you ride the **Palm Springs Aerial Tramway,** almost 5,000ft (1,524m) straight up. This is the perfect way to escape the debilitating summer heat. The tram climbs up to the wooded trails and campgrounds at the top, where welcoming refreshments are available.

 11X

Anza-Borrego Desert State Park

✉ Visitors Center, 2 miles (3.2km) west of Borrego Springs Township

☎ 760/767-4205; www.parks.ca.gov

🕓 Oct–May daily 9–5; Jun–Sep Sat–Sun 9–5 💷 Inexpensive

Agua Caliente Indian Reservation

☎ 760/323-0151 🕓 Wed–Sat 10–5, Sun noon–5 (shorter hours in summer)

💷 Inexpensive

Palm Springs Aerial Tramway
✉ Tramway Road, 3 miles (5km) southwest of SR 111 ☎ 760/325-1391; www.pstramway.com 🕐 Mon–Fri 10–8, Sat–Sun 8–8. Closed 2 weeks in Aug ✋ Expensive

PALOMAR MOUNTAIN STATE PARK
Palomar Observatory houses the famous 200in (513cm) Hale telescope. High above the city lights, the observatory also has smaller telescopes, used to monitor the planet's movement. The small Greenway Museum contains photographs of the observatory's celestial sightings. There are spectacular views of the Pacific from the park.

➕ 11Y ✉ 40 miles (65km) northeast of San Diego on SR 6 ☎ 760/742-3462; www.parks.ca.gov 🕐 Dawn–dusk ✋ Inexpensive; parking fee

RIVERSIDE
Because the region has the ideal climate and soil for growing navel oranges, this was the wealthiest US city per capita and the metropolitan center of Southern California at the turn of the 20th century. Several buildings remain from around this time: the Italian Renaissance-style City Hall, the Classic Revival municipal museum, and many exquisite Victorian homes. In addition, mission architecture and adobe residences still reflect the early wealth and prestige.

California Citrus State Historic Park preserves some of the rapidly vanishing landscape of the citrus industry and features a grove of 80 varieties of citrus trees. The visitor center is located in a Victorian house. The Riverside Municipal Museum, at 3720 Orange Street, traces the history of citrus-growing in the region.

➕ 10W

California Citrus State Historic Park
✉ 9400 Dufferin Avenue ☎ 951/780-6222; www.parks.ca.gov 🕐 Daily 8–5 (until 7 Apr–Sep); visitor center Wed, Sat, Sun 10–4 ✋ Inexpensive; parking fee 🍴 Picnic facilities

SAN DIEGO

San Diego rarely gets rain, never freezes, has an average annual daytime temperature between 58 and 70°F (14 and 21°C), and more than 70 miles (113km) of sandy beaches. California's second largest city, it retains a small-town ambience. Ralph Waldo Emerson must have visited San Diego when he said "California has better days and more of them."

➕ 11Z

Balboa Park

Best places to see, pages 36–37.

The Beaches

The most popular of the city's beaches is Pacific Beach (known as "PB" by the locals), which features The Tourmaline Surfing Park, a surfer's paradise. Mission Beach has a 3-mile (5km) walk of shops and skateboard, rollerblade and bicycle rental stands. Ocean Beach is one of the liveliest in San Diego, and a good place to fish. Point Loma is an upscale beach, with spectacular views of the naval ships' comings and goings.

Cabrillo National Monument

A 144-acre (58ha) park along steep cliffs, Cabrillo rewards with great views of San Diego Bay, and it's an especially good place to spot gray whales migrating to Mexico between mid-December and mid-March. The Old Point Loma Lighthouse, dating from 1855, is 25 miles (43km) out to sea, but visible from here on a clear day.

✉ 10 miles (16km) west of I–8 on Catalina Boulevard ☎ 619/557-5450; www.nps.gov/cabr 🕐 Daily 9–5 💵 Inexpensive

Coronado Island

A combination of wealthy enclave and naval base, Coronado sits just across the bay from downtown San Diego. The easiest way to reach it is on the Bay Ferry. Leaving from Broadway Pier downtown, the ferry arrives at Old Ferry Landing in Coronado in 15 minutes. You can also reach the island via the towering San Diego–Coronado Bay Bridge (toll). The main attraction on the island is Hotel Del Coronado (➤ 178). A testament to the beauty of Victorian architecture, the "Del" was opened in 1888, and film buffs might remember it as one of the main locations in Marilyn Monroe's film *Some Like It Hot*.

📧 619/234-4111; inexpensive
ℹ 1100 Orange Avenue; tel: 619/437-8788; Mon–Fri 9–5, Sat–Sun 10–5

Gaslamp Quarter

The reclamation of San Diego's 19th-century Gaslamp Quarter is one of urban America's great success stories. After having been slated for demolition, many of its Victorian-era cast-iron and other buildings were restored and converted into stores, restaurants and nightclubs, and the area is now the center of San Diego's vibrant nightlife.

www.gaslamp.org

House of Pacific Relations

The culture and art of 31 nations is housed in the museum's 15 California/Spanish-style cottages located in the Pan American Plaza. Other Plaza attractions are the Aerospace Museum, San Diego Automotive Museum and the open-air Starlight Bowl.

www.sdhpr.org

✉ 2125 Park Boulevard, Balboa Park ☎ 619/234-0739 🕐 Sun noon–5, 4th Tue in month 11–3

✋ Free; donations welcome

La Jolla

Pronounced *La Hoya* (Spanish for "The Jewel"), this picturesque cove, just north of San Diego, is one of the prettiest places in the whole state. This unspoiled piece of coastline offers expensive restaurants and boutiques on its two main thoroughfares: Prospect Street and Girard Avenue. Just north of La Jolla are the equally scenic towns of Del Mar and Solana Beach. Relatively undiscovered by tourists, these beaches epitomize the beauty and tranquility of Southern California.

✉ 10 miles (16km) north of San Diego via I-805 or Highway 1

167

Maritime Museum of San Diego

A total of 10 vessels complement the museum displays. The pick of the bunch is the 1863 *Star of India*, a fully equipped three-mast sailing ship, the oldest iron-hulled ship in America still afloat. San Francisco's *Berkeley* was the ferry used to evacuate victims of the 1906 earthquake. The 1904 steam-powered yacht *Medea* occasionally sails around the Bay.

www.sdmaritime.org

✉ 1492 North Harbor Drive ☎ 619/234-9153 🕓 Daily 9–8 (closes 9pm in summer) ✋ Moderate

Mission Bay Park

There are miles of cycling paths throughout this huge aquatic park, and a bicycle rental stand can be found just off East Mission Bay Drive. Kite flying and volleyball are popular pastimes here, and watersports, as well as golf, picnicking and camping, can be found. The park is also the home of Sea World (▶ 173). Next to the park is Fiesta Island, popular for jet skiing and "over the line" baseball.

🕓 Daily ✋ Free ℹ 2688 E Mission Bay Drive; tel: 619/276-8200

Museum of Man

The San Diego Museum of Man, located below the California Tower (➤ 36), offers eclectic, ever-changing exhibits from Californians and Hopi tribes, ancient Egypt and mummies, to the Maya and early man.

www.museumofman.org

✉ 1350 El Prado Drive ☎ 619/239-2001 🕐 Daily 10–4:30 ✋ Inexpensive

Old Town San Diego State Historic Park

The remains of the first European settlement in California, Old Town is preserved with National Park status. The most important area is the Mission San Diego de Alcala, California's first mission, founded in 1769 by Father Junípero Serra. Restored and still used for services, it has beautiful gardens and adobe structures and houses the Museum de Luis Jayme. One of the oldest buildings, Casa de Estudillo, has survived several hundred years. Old Town Plaza was a meeting place and center for festivals, religious celebrations and even bullfights in the mid-1800s. Here you'll find the visitors' center, where you can join free tours of the grounds.

✉ San Diego Avenue, at Twiggs Street ☎ 619/220-5422; www.parks.ca.gov
🕐 Visitors' center daily 10–5; park always open ✋ Free

Presidio Park

Formerly the fort here protected Mission San Diego de Alcala. The park is up the hill from the center of Old Town. As you sit on the benches scattered among the trees of this 50-acre (20ha) park you will have wonderful views of the Old Town expanse. San Diego's landmark museum, the Junipero Serra, sits high atop the hill where California's first mission and presidio were founded. Spanish, Mexican and Native American aspects of San Diego's history are recalled with exhibits of furniture, clothing, household items and other artifacts of the past 200 years.

✉ 2727 Presidio Drive ☎ 619/297-3258 🕐 Park daily; Junipero Serra Museum daily 10–4:30 ✋ Inexpensive

a walk around San Diego

**Starting at the Old Town visitors'
center, you pass historic
buildings, museums and sites that
encompass the oldest and most
beautiful part of San Diego.**

*From the visitors' center, walk
southward and turn east on San Diego
Avenue, continuing to the Machado-
Silvas Adobe house.*

This is one of the more famous buildings
built in the mid-19th century, and houses
the Courthouse and the Colorado
House/Wells Fargo Museum.

*After touring the house, continue a
short distance north to Mason Street.*

Here you will see the Mason Street
School. Built in 1865, this one-room
building was San Diego's first publicly
owned school.

*Continue north on Mason to San
Diego Avenue, then turn east to
Dodson's Corner.*

Dodson's Corner is a group of false-front
shops where merchants sometimes
dress in period costume. Across San
Diego Avenue is the San Diego Union
Museum, home of the state's longest
running newspaper.

From here go north on Twiggs Street to Calhoun Street.

At Calhoun you will see the Steely Stables, and Blackhawk Smith and Stable, both worth a look.

Walk west on Calhoun to the Alvarado House and Johnson House, two beautiful and historic structures. Retrace your steps back to Mason Street, then head south to visit the Casa De Estudillo. After touring the Casa, step across the street back into Old Town Plaza to end your tour.

To complement your stroll through Old Town, you could visit the nearby Gaslamp Quarter, bound by Broadway, 4th, 6th and Harbor streets, which gives a comprehensive history of San Diego's architecture.

Distance 3.5 miles (5.5km)
Time 3 hours
Start point Visitors' center, Old Town State Historic Park
End point Old Town Plaza
Lunch Miguel's ($), 2444 San Diego Avenue; tel: 619/298-9840; www.brigantine.com; Mon–Sat 11–9:30, Sun 4–9

San Diego Zoo Safari Park

The safari park, 30 miles (48km) northeast of San Diego, is known
for its authentic re-creation of African and Asian terrain. Almost
2,500 endangered animals are presented here by the Zoological
Society of San Diego. This 2,100-acre (850ha) preserve features a
monorail tour, Nairobi Village animal shows, hiking trails and
botanical exhibits.

www.sandiegozoo.org/park

✉ Via Rancho Pkwy exit off I–15 ☎ 619/234-6541 🕓 Daily from 9am,
closing times vary 💰 Expensive (combination pass with San Diego Zoo)

Scripps Oceanography and Birch Aquarium

Part of the University of California at San Diego, Birch Aquarium and the Memorial Pier are landmarks of the La Jolla coast. Marine scientists have been working here since the turn of the century. The Institute displays the aquatic world in indoor tanks, an on-shore tidepool and through additional oceanographic exhibits showing the latest advances in oceanography.

www.sio.ucsd.edu; aquarium.ucsd.edu

✉ 2300 Expedition Way ☎ 858/534-3474 ⊙ Daily 9–5 🖐 Moderate

SeaWorld

Perhaps one of, if not *the* finest marine biology park in the world, SeaWorld is impressive, and you can and should plan on spending the better part of a day here. Comfortably spread out over 150 acres (61ha), it features continuous killer whale and dolphin shows, and highly informative marine life exhibits. Between shows, you can touch or view live animals in the petting pools. Also not to miss are the nautical theme playground, marina and state-of-the-art research laboratories.

SeaWorld is home to killer whales Shamu and Baby Shamu, the real stars of the park, as well as seals, sea lions and walruses. The Rocky Point Preserve is a habitat for dolphins and sea otters, while "Penguin Encounter" has over 300 penguins. Other exhibits include "Pets Rule!" and "Fools with Tools." A family-oriented theme park features interactive games and adventures. Guided tours are available, and in the summer there are evening aquatic shows. Owing to the park's popularity, you can expect long waits for some shows and exhibits, especially during the summer. Don't forget the re-entry stamp if you decide to leave the park and return later. Ticket sales stop 90 minutes before closing, which is around sunset most of the year, but up until 11pm in the summer.

www.seaworld.com

✉ SeaWorld Drive off the I–5, Mission Bay Park ☎ 619/226-3901 ⊙ Daily from 10am, closing times vary with season 🖐 Expensive

a walk in Sequoia National Park

This walk takes you through the forest of Sequoia National Park. Even if you visit during the heat of the summer, you will find the temperatures comfortably cool because of the towering foliage.

Begin at the General Sherman Tree, 2 miles (3.2km) east of Giant Forest Village.

The General Sherman tree (named for the Civil War general) is 275ft (84m) high. It is estimated to be more than 2,500 years old and contains enough wood to build at least 40 houses.

Walk down the self-guided, paved Congress Trail. Cross Sherman Creek on the quaint wooden bridge.

Experience the awesome giant sequoias, like the character-laden Leaning Tree and some lightning-struck and fire-scarred trees as well.

About a mile (1.6km) further, you will meet the junction with the Alta Trail and a grove known as The Senate. A little further along the fern-filled trail is The House Grove.

These two stands are named after the two governing bodies of the United States government. The path also visits the McKinley Tree (named for the US president). After World War II, the practice of naming big trees after politicos was abandoned.

Continue a half-mile (0.8km) back, and return to the trail head. For a longer hike (about 6 miles/10km), follow the Congress Trail to the junction of The Trail of the Sequoias. Take this path for a half-mile (0.8km) to the hike's high point, then gradually descend one and a half miles (2.5km) into Long Meadow.

Lunch before, or after, your hike at Giant Forest Village.

Distance 5 miles (8km)
Time 2–4 hours
Start point General Sherman Tree
End point General Sherman or Long Meadow
Lunch Grant Grove Restaurant ($$), Grant Grove Visitors Center; tel: 559/335-5500, ext 306

SIMI VALLEY

The main reason for visiting Simi Valley is to see the **Ronald Reagan Presidential Library,** set in a beautiful, Spanish mission-style, hilltop mansion. Among the exhibits are photographs and memorabilia of the former US president's life, a full-scale replica of the Oval Office and a large segment of the Berlin Wall.

➕ 9W

Ronald Reagan Presidential Library

✉ 40 Presidential Drive ☎ 800/410-8354; www.reaganlibrary.com ⏱ Daily 10–5 💰 Moderate

SOLEDAD

Soledad, the oldest settlement in the Salinas Valley, was established in 1791 with the founding of **Mission Nuestra Señora de la Soledad**. The ruins of this adobe mission, along with a restored chapel and museum, can be seen to the east of town.

➕ 5K

Mission Nuestra Senora de la Soledad

✉ Fort Romie Road ☎ 831/678-2586 ⏱ Daily 10–4 💰 Donations

HOTELS

BIG BEAR LAKE
▽▽▽ Apples Bed & Breakfast Inn ($$)
A secluded setting close to shops and recreation. The lovingly decorated rooms are all named after apples.

✉ 42439 Moonridge Road ☎ 909/866-0903; www.applesbigbear.com

CATALINA ISLAND
▽▽▽ Hotel Metropole ($$)
There are magnificent ocean views from the hotel's rooftop sun deck and spa.

✉ 205 Crescent Avenue, Avalon ☎ 310/510-1884; www.hotel-metropole.com

▽▽▽ Hotel Vista Del Mar ($$)
Resort hotel overlooking the beach with larger, comfortable rooms; most with spectacular views.

✉ 417 Crescent Avenue, Avalon ☎ 310/510-1452; www.hotel-vistadelmar.com

DEATH VALLEY
▽▽▽ The Inn at Furnace Creek ($$$)
Stay in Native American decor, built in the 1920s, and choose between luxurious motel-style rooms and furnished cabins.

✉ Call or visit website for directions ☎ 760/786-2345; www.furnacecreekresort.com 🕑 Oct–May only

LAKE ARROWHEAD
▽▽▽ Romantique Lakeview Lodge ($)
Set in wooded land near the lake, this quaint lodge has cozy rooms at affordable rates, especially during the week.

✉ 28051 Highway 189 ☎ 800/358-5253; www.lakeviewlodge.com

ORANGE COUNTY
▽▽▽▽ The Island Hotel Newport Beach ($$$)
One of the finest hotels in the state in a contemporary design with a tree-lined swimming pool and tennis courts.

✉ 690 Newport Center Drive, Newport Beach ☎ 949/759-0808; www.theislandhotel.com

PALM SPRINGS
🏵🏵 Casa Cody Inn ($$–$$$)
This welcoming B&B offers a range of rooms in a historic house set in leafy grounds, as well as filling gourmet breakfasts.
✉ 175 S Cahuilla Road ☎ 760/320-3296; www.casacody.com

SAN DIEGO
🏵🏵🏵 Bay Club Hotel ($$)
Large rooms, some with private balconies and patios, situated on the Marina with excellent views of boating activity.
✉ 2131 Shelter Island Drive ☎ 619/224-8888; www.bayclubhotel.com

🏵🏵 Comfort Inn Gaslamp ($$)
In the historic Gaslamp Quarter, and close to the zoo and Balboa Park. The rooms are of the usual chain standard.
✉ 660 G Street ☎ 619/238-4100; www.comfortinngaslamp.com

🏵🏵🏵 Horton Grand ($$)
The oldest building in San Diego (1886), the Horton Grand has Victorian decor with an impressive lobby.
✉ 311 Island Avenue ☎ 619/544-1886; www.hortongrand.com

🏵🏵 🏵🏵 Hotel del Coronado ($$$)
Famous Victorian hotel from the 1880s, jutting out into the bay, with large rooms and some suites. One room is "haunted."
✉ 1500 Orange Avenue ☎ 619/435-6611; www.hoteldel.com

🏵🏵🏵 Humphrey's ($$)
Relax in beautiful gardens and island decor while admiring great views looking out over the bay.
✉ 2241 Shelter Island Drive ☎ 619/224-3577; www.humphreysbythebay.com

🏵🏵🏵🏵 The Lodge at Torrey Pines ($$$)
Luxurious five-star accommodations in La Jolla in well-crafted wooden buildings. Fantastic ocean views.
✉ 11480 North Torrey Pines Road ☎ 858/453-4420; www.lodgetorreypines.com

RESTAURANTS

BARSTOW
✦✦ Los Domingo's ($)
Wonderful, authentic Mexican food in a no-frills setting that makes an ideal pit stop if you're en route to Las Vegas from LA. Excellent, efficient service.

✉ 1520 E Main Street ☎ 760/256-1381 🕙 Daily 6am–midnight

BIG BEAR LAKE
✦✦ Mill Creek Manor Tea Room ($)
A delicious array of hot and cold gourmet sandwiches are available, as well as teas, cakes and other sweet and savory delights, at this homey rustic retreat.

✉ 39904 Big Bear Boulevard ☎ 909/866-8066 🕙 Daily 11–5

LAKE ARROWHEAD
✦✦✦ Bin 189 ($$)
Located in the delightful Lake Arrowhead Resort, with an elevated view of the lake, this restaurant offers a range of sandwiches, salads, meat dishes and tempting desserts.

✉ 27984 Highway 189 ☎ 909/336-1511; www.laresort.com 🕙 Sun–Thu 7am–9pm, Fri–Sat 7–10

ORANGE COUNTY
✦✦✦✦ 21 Oceanfront ($$$)
A charming steak and seafood restaurant at the foot of Newport Pier, with great sunset views. Efficient staff are always willing to help with your wine choice.

✉ 2100 W Oceanfront, Newport Beach ☎ 949/673-2100; www.21oceanfront.com 🕙 Sun–Thu 5–10, Fri–Sat 5–11

✦✦✦✦ Antonello Ristorante ($$)
Since 1979 this local favorite has been serving Northern Italian fare in a rustic, elegant setting. The *cioppino* is a veritable feast of mixed seafood.

✉ 3800 Plaza Drive, Santa Ana ☎ 714/751-7153; www.antonello.com 🕙 Mon–Fri 11:30–2, 5–9:30, Sat 5–10

▼▼▼ Bistango ($$$)

This combination of restaurant and art gallery offers varied Continental cuisine, prix fixe, accompanied by an extensive wine list and nightly entertainment.

✉ 19100 Von Karman Avenue, Irvine ☎ 949/752-5222; www.bistango.com
🕐 Mon–Fri 11:30–2:30, 5:30–9:30 (until 10:30 Fri), Sat 5:30–10:30

▼▼▼ Chakra Cuisine ($$)

Dishes from all over India feature at this place. Try the spicy lamb Hyderabadi or the Goan shrimp curry.

✉ 4143 Campus Drive, Irvine ☎ 949/854-0009; www.chakracuisine.com
🕐 Sun–Thu 11:30–10, Fri–Sat 11:30–11

▼▼ The Olde Ship ($$)

This British pub gathers ex-pats for the beer and TV soccer, while everyone loves the traditional UK food such as roast beef and Yorkshire pudding.

✉ 1120 W 17th Street, Santa Ana ☎ 714/550-6700; www.theoldeship.com
🕐 Daily 11–11

▼▼▼ Studio ($$$)

On a bluff overlooking the ocean, this is a dream location for dining on the excellent California/French cuisine or just sipping a cocktail.

✉ 30801 Coast Highway, Laguna Beach ☎ 949/715-6420;
www.studiolagunabeach.com 🕐 Wed–Sun 5–10

▼▼▼ Yard House ($$)

This low-key nationwide chain provides an above average variety of American favorites from burgers to jerk chicken.

✉ 849 Newport Center Drive, Newport Beach ☎ 949/640-9273;
www.yardhouse.com 🕐 Daily 11–11

▼▼ Yi-Dynasty ($$)

Massive shared portions of specialties such as *saeng deung sim*, which consists of rib-eye, make up the menu at this Korean BBQ.

✉ 1701 Corinthian Way, Newport Beach ☎ 949/797-9292;
www.yi-dynasty.com 🕐 Mon–Fri 11–10, Sat noon–10

▼▼▼ Zov's Bistro ($$)

Trendy spot with imaginative Mediterranean cuisine and fresh bread from the on-site bakery.

✉ 17740 E 17th Street, Tustin ☎ 714/838-8855; www.zovs.com ⏰ Mon–Fri 11–2, 5–9:30, Sat 5–10

PALM SPRINGS/PALM DESERT

▼▼ Las Casuelas Terraza ($)

Mexican food and fantastic margaritas in a relaxing but lively atmosphere. The combination of platters are well worth it.

✉ 222 South Palm Canyon Drive, Palm Springs ☎ 760/325-2794; www.lascasuelas.com ⏰ Daily 11–10

▼▼▼ Cork Tree ($$$)

The elegant dining room and romantic patio offer alternative scenes to enjoy the high-quality California cuisine that is served at Cork Tree.

✉ 74-950 Country Club Drive, Palm Desert ☎ 760/779-0123; www.thecorktree.com ⏰ Mon–Fri 11–2, 5–10, Sat 5–10

▼▼▼ Cuistot ($$$)

A popular and elegant restaurant featuring California–French cuisine. The specialties are veal and rack of lamb.

✉ 72-595 El Paseo, Palm Desert ☎ 760/340-1000; www.cuistotrestaurant.com ⏰ Tue–Sat 11:30–2:30, 5:30–10, Sun 5:30–10

▼▼▼ Palm Springs Chop House ($$$)

Steaks, chops and large side orders and tasty desserts stand out here, but the Colorado lamb rack is a real treat, too.

✉ 262 S Palm Canyon Drive, Palm Springs ☎ 760/320-4500; www.restaurantofplamsprings.com ⏰ Daily 5–10

▼▼▼ Ristorante Mamma Gina ($$)

This authentic northern Italian offers homemade pasta, and popular chicken and veal specialties.

✉ 73–705 El Paseo Drive, Palm Desert ☎ 760/568-9898; www.mammagina.com ⏰ Mon–Sat 11:30–2, 4:30–10

▼▼▼ La Spiga ($$)

Popular Italian restaurant in a Tuscan villa-style building. The Sicilian chef rustles up tasty dishes from various parts of Italy.

✉ 72-557 Highway 111, Palm Desert ☎ 760/340-9318; www.laspigapalmdesert.com ⏰ Mon–Sat 5:30–9:30

▼▼▼ Spencer's Restaurant ($$)

Treats like American paddlefish caviar are among the unusual fare on offer at this place that presents California cuisine with a touch of flair.

✉ 701 W Baristo Road, Palm Springs ☎ 760/327-3446; www.spencersrestaurant.com ⏰ Daily 9–2:30, 5:30–10

SAN DIEGO

▼ Anthony's Fish Grotto ($$$)

Family-owned seafood restaurant with beautiful harbor views. Steak and chicken also available.

✉ 1360 Harbor Drive ☎ 619/232-5103; www.gofishanthonys.com ⏰ Daily 11–2:30, 4:30–10

▼▼▼ Candelas ($$$)

This trendy Mexican restaurant offers high-quality food in an intimate setting with romantic lighting and snazzy music.

✉ 416 Third Avenue ☎ 619/702-4455; www.candelas-sd.com ⏰ Daily 5–11, brunch Sat–Sun 8:30–2

▼ City Delicatessen ($)

Centrally located Jewish deli where you can tuck into hearty portions of breakfast, lunch or dinner. There's also a fine bakery.

✉ 535 University Avenue ☎ 619/295-2747; www.citydeli.com ⏰ Sun–Thu 7am–midnight, Fri–Sat 7am–2am

▼▼▼ Grant Grill ($$)

Popular downtown grill, whose setting in the famous 1910 hotel of the same name, adds a sprig of class to the succulent meat served.

✉ 326 Broadway ☎ 619/744-2077; www.grantgrill.com ⏰ Sun–Thu 8am–10pm, Fri–Sat 8am–10:30pm

♦♦ Hob Nob Hill ($)

Family-owned and open since World War II, the specialties include fried scallops and rack of lamb. Kids' menu. Great for breakfast.

✉ 2271 First Avenue (near Balboa Park) ☎ 619/239-8176; www.hobnobhill.com 🕐 Daily 7–9

♦♦♦ Trattoria La Strada ($$)

The oven roasted leg of lamb with herbs and cognac is just one of the specialties available at this established downtown Italian.

✉ 702 Fifth Avenue ☎ 619/239-3400 🕐 Daily 11:30–11

♦♦♦ Umi Sushi ($$)

Traditional sushi offerings, plus tempura, teriyaki and specials. It also does a fine line in sashimi salads.

✉ 2806 Shelter Island Drive ☎ 619/226-1135; www.umisushisandiego.com
🕐 Mon–Sat 11:30–2:30, 5–10, Sun 5–10

SHOPPING

ART AND ANTIQUES
Antique Row

More than 20 dealers give this street its name.

✉ Adams Avenue, Kensington, San Diego

BOOKS
Mysterious Galaxy

Bookshop for suspense, horror, science fiction and the occult fans.

✉ 7051 Claremont Mesa Road, San Diego ☎ 858/268-4747

FACTORY OUTLETS
Las Americas Premium Outlets

The mega-complex contains 125 outlets covering a vast range.

✉ 4211 Las Camino de Plaza, San Diego ☎ 619/934-8400; www.premiumoutlets.com

Lake Arrowhead Village

Fifteen outlets in a beautiful setting by the lake.

✉ Shoreline, Lake Arrowhead ☎ 909/337-2533; www.lakearrowhead.com

Barstow Outlets
Convenient location en route to Death Valley, with over 20 stores.
✉ Lenwood Road, off I–15, Barstow ☎ 760/253-7342;
www.barstowoutlets.com

FASHION
The Paladion
Posh center with Cartier, Tiffany's, Gucci and more.
✉ 777 Front Street, San Diego ☎ 619/232-1627

ENTERTAINMENT

NIGHTLIFE
Belly Up
With live acts ranging from old folkies to jazz legends, as well as
top DJs, this joint attracts all sorts from around San Diego.
✉ 143 S Cedros Avenue, Solana Beach ☎ 858/481-8140;
www.bellyup.com

The Casbah
See page 70.

Top O' the Cove
Piano bar/restaurant featuring show tunes and standards in a great
location with great views.
✉ 1216 Prospect Street, La Jolla ☎ 858/454-7779; www.topofthecove.com

Zelda's Nightclub
State-of-the-art club with a dresscode for lovers of hip-hop, r'n'b
and other dance genres.
✉ 611 S Palm Canyon Drive, Palm Springs ☎ 760/325-2375;
www.newzeldasnightclub.com

PERFORMING ARTS
Civic Theatre
Ultramodern design provides a great backdrop to concerts held
here, from classical to jazz. Hosts comedy, too.
✉ 1110 Third Avenue, San Diego ☎ 619/615-4100; www.sandiegotheatres.org

La Jolla Playhouse

La Jolla puts on a range of plays from Shakespeare to musicals and avant garde.

✉ 2910 La Jolla Village Drive, La Jolla ☎ 858/550-1010; www.lajollaplayhouse.org

Orange County Performing Arts Center

Regular performances by New York City Opera, American Ballet Theater and Los Angeles Philharmonic Orchestra, plus presentations of popular musicals.

✉ 600 Town Center Drive, Costa Mesa ☎ 714/556-2787; www.ocpac.org

Sledgehammer Theatre

Avant-garde productions in a converted funeral parlor.

✉ 1620 Sixth Avenue, San Diego ☎ 619/544-1484; www.sledgehammer.org

Welk Resort Theatre

Dinner theater, with Broadway and Broadway-style shows. Buffet matinee and evening.

✉ 8860 Lawrence Welk Drive, Escondido ☎ 888/802-7469; www.welktheatersandiego.com

SPORTS

Eldorado Polo Club

The "Winter Polo Capital of the West." Weekday practice matches are free here and there are designated picnic grounds.

✉ 50–950 Madison Street, Indio ☎ 760/342-2223; www.elderadopolo.com

Palm Springs Tennis Center

Nine lit courts are open to the public.

✉ 1300 Baristo Road, Palm Springs ☎ 760/320-0020

Westin Mission Hills Resort Golf Club

This golf resort is one good reason why Palm Springs is "Winter Golf Capital of the World".

✉ 71333 Dinah Shore Drive, Rancho Mirage, Palm Springs ☎ 760/328-3198; www.westinmissionhillsgolf.com

Index

Acknowledgements

The Automobile Association wishes to thank the following photographers, companies and picture libraries for their assistance in the preparation of this book.
Abbreviations for the picture credits are as follows – (t) top; (b) bottom; (l) left; (r) right; (c) centre; (AA) AA World Travel Library.

4l Hollywood Sign, AA/C Sawyer; **4c** Looking over harbour freeway, in Los Angeles, AA/Anna Mockford & Nick Bonetti; **4r** Monterey Bay, AA/R Ireland; **5l** Surfers on Surf Rider Beach in Malibu, AA/ AA/Anna Mockford & Nick Bonetti; **5c** Russian Hill, San Francisco, AA/K Paterson; **6/7** Hollywood Sign, AA/C Sawyer; **8/9** Vernal Fall, Yosemite, National Park, AA/R Ireland; **10//11t** Skaters at Venice Beach, AA/C Sawyer; **10ct** Redwoods State Park, Santa Cruz Mountain, AA/K Paterson; **10cb** Sterling Wineries, San Francisco, AA/K Paterson; **10bl** Joshua Tree National Monument Park, Imagestate; **10br** Cascade Lake, Lake Tahoe, AA/R Ireland; **11c** Otani's Hotel Garden in the Sky, Little Tokyo, Los Angeles, AA/M Jourdan; **11b** Beverley Hills Hotel, Sunset Boulevard, Los Angeles, AA/C Sawyer; **12/13t** Grand Central Marks, Los Angeles, AA/M Jourdan; **12bl** Fredericks of Hollywood, Hollywood Boulevard, AA/M Jourdan; **12br** Burger in Pasadena Cafe, AA/ AA/Anna Mockford & Nick Bonetti; **13t** Fisherman's Wharf, San Francisco. AA/B Smith; **13b** Waiter at restaurant on Chestnut Street, San Francisco, AA/C Sawyer; **14t** Café on Columbus Avenue, San Francisco, AA/C Sawyer; **14/15** Sterling Vineyards, Napa Valley, AA/K Paterson; **15t** Grand Central Market, Los Angeles, AA/M Jourdan; **15c** Mel's Diner, AA/M Jourdan; **15b** Yabu's restaurant, Little Tokyo, Los Angeles, AA/M Jourdan; **16** Getty Center, South Promontory, Los Angeles, AA/M Jourdan; **16** Mariposa Grove, Yosemite National Park, AA/R Ireland; **17c** Ride at Knotts Berry Farm, Courtesy of AOCVCB/Knotts Berry Farm; **17bl** Commuters on evening ferry to Sausalito, with Golden Gate Bridge, San Francisco, AA/K Paterson; **17br** Billboard, Sunset Boulevard, AA/C Sawyer; **18/19t** Vineyard, St Helena, Napa Valley, AA/H Harris; **18/19b** Huntington Beach, surfer, AA/C Sawyer; **19** Woman walking along the Walk of Fame, Hollywood, Los Angeles, AA/M Jourdan; **20/21** Looking over harbour freeway, in Los Angeles, AA/Anna Mockford & Nick Bonetti; **24/25** Memorial Day Parade, San Diego, AA/M Jourdan; **26/27** Portal Railway Museum, AA/R Ireland; **28** View of Tour Thru Tree, AA/R Ireland; **29** Policeman, AA/C Sawyer; **34/35** Monterey Bay, AA/R Ireland; **36/37** California Building in Copley Park. Balboa Park; **38/9** Catalina Island, Harbour and Casino, © Rob Crandall/Alamy; **40/41** Disneyland® Resort, © Disney. Photo: Paul Hiffmeyer; **42** Golden Gate Bridge, San Francisco, AA/K Paterson; **43** Golden Gate Bridge from estuary, AA/K Paterson; **44/45** Hearst Castle from the air, Hearst Castle; **45** Hearst Castle, main library, Hearst Castle; **46** Hollywood Walk of Fame, Los Angeles, AA/C Sawyer; **47** Hollywood Sign, AA/P Wilson; **48** Monterey Bay Aquarium, AA/R Ireland; **48/49** Monterey Bay, AA/R Ireland; **50/51** Yosemite Valley from Tunnel View, Yosemite National Park, AA/R Ireland; **51** Villa Sattiu winery, Napa Valley; **AA/H Harris; 52** Big Basin Redwoods State Park, AA/K Paterson; **52/53** Redwood Tree, Redwoods State Park, AA/K Paterson; **54** Yosemite Falls, Yosemite National Park, AA/R Ireland; **54/55** El Capitan Cathedral Rocks, Yosemite National Park, AA/R Ireland; **56/57** Surfers on Surf Rider Beach in Malibu, AA/ AA/Anna Mockford & Nick Bonetti; **58/59** People outside 'Dotties' True Blue Café, San Francisco, © Kumar Sriskandan/Alamy; **60** Annual Snow Festival, Snow Festival/North Lake Tahoe, **62/63** Shopping on Rodeo Drive, Beverley hills, AA/C Sawyer; **64** Golden Gate Bridge, AA/K Paterson; **66/67** Manhatten Beach, Los Angeles, AA/C Sawyer; **69** Fairground, Santa Monica, AA/P Wilson; **71** People dancing in a club, Brand X Pics; **72/3** View from Mulholland Drive in Hollywood, Los Angeles, AA/Anna Mockford & Nick Bonetti; **73t** Venice Beach, Canal, Los Angeles, AA/M Jourdan; **73b** Malibu number plate, AA/C Sawyer; **74/75** Russian Hill, San Francisco, AA/K Paterson; **77** San Francisco Museum of Modern Art, AA/K Paterson; **78t** Cell in Alcatraz, AA/H Harris; **78b** Ferry in San Francisco Bay, AA/K Paterson; **79** Eastern Indian Gallery at the Asian Art Museum, Kaz Tsuruta/Asian Art Museum, San Francisco; **80** View inside Rainforest Dome looking down into Amazon Flooded Forest Tank, California Academy of Sciences, Tim Griffith; **81** Palace of the Legion of Honor, San Francisco, AA/K Paterson; **83** Fisherman's Wharf sign, San Francisco, AA/K Paterson; **84** Chinatown Gate, San Francisco, AA/K Paterson; **85** Lantern, Chinatown, San Francisco, AA/K Paterson; **86** Grace Episcopal Cathedral, San Francisco, AA/K Paterson; **86/87** Hyde Street Pier, San Francisco, AA/K Paterson; **87** Lombard Street, San Francisco, AA/B Smith; **88/89** Mission Dolores, San Francisco, AA/K Paterson; **89** Palace of Fine Arts, AA/K Paterson; **90** Museum of Modern Art, San Francisco, AA/K Paterson; **90/91** Transamerica Pyramid, AA/K Paterson; **91** Wells Fargo Museum, AA/K Paterson; **99** Pine Ridge Winery, AA/H Harris; **100/101** Victorian House, Eureka, © F1 online digitale Bildagentur GmbH/Alamy; **103** Auburn, statue of gold miner, © David Sanger Photography/Alamy; **104** Lake Tahoe, AA/R Ireland; **104/105** Lassen Volcanic Park, AA/R Ireland; **106/107** Shasta National Forest, AA/R Ireland; **108/109t** Treasure Island Marina, San Francisco, AA/B Smith; **108/109b** Treasure Island, AA/K Paterson; **110/111** Sacramento Street, San Francisco, AA/K Paterson; **111** Rosicrucian Egyptian Museum, San Jose, AA/K Paterson; **112/113** Rosicrucian Egyptian Museum, San Jose, AA/K Paterson; **113** Winery, St Helena, Napa Valley, AA/K Paterson; **114/115** Pine Ridge Winery, Napa Valley, AA/H Harris; **121** Santa Barbara, AA/C Sawyer; **122/123** Carmel Beach at Sunset, AA/R Ireland; **124** Paseo Neuvo Center, Santa Barbara, AA/C Sawyer; **125** Santa Barbara, AA/C Sawyer; **126/127** Solvang, Alamy, © David Muscroft; **131** Chinatown, Los Angeles, AA/M Jourdan; **132** Sunset Boulevard Sign, Los Angeles, AA/M Jourdan; **132/133** Beverley Hills, Los Angeles, AA/M Jourdan; **133** City Hall, Old Pasadena, Los Angeles, AA/P Wilson; **134t** Beverley Hills Hotel, AA; **134b** Vermont and Sunset Metro Stations, Los Angeles, AA/M Jourdan; **135** Shopping, Rodeo Drive, AA/C Sawyer; **136** Natural History Museum, Los Angeles, AA/M Jourdan; **137t** Stan Laurel Memorial Stone, Los Angeles, AA/P Wilson; **136/137** Central Garden, Getty Center, AA/M Jourdan; **138** Statue of James Dean, Los Angeles, AA/M Jourdan; **138/139t** Huntington Library, Los Angeles, AA/P Wilson; **138/139b** Little Tokyo, Los Angeles, AA/M Jourdan; **140** Long Beach Shoreline Village, AA/C Sawyer; **141** Mann's Chinese Theatre, Los Angeles, AA/M Jourdan; **142/143** Venice Beach, Los Angeles, AA/M Jourdan; **153** Death Valley National Monument, Imagestate; **154** Bakersfield Kern County Museum & Pioneer Village, historic doctors office building, © Stephen Saks Photography/Alamy; **156/157t** Death Valley National Monument, Brand X Pictures; **156/157b** Joshua Tree National Park, Imagestate; **158/159** Orange County Sunset, Courtesy of Anaheim/Orange Country Visitor and Convention Bureau; **160/161** Mission San Juan Capistrano, AA/P Wood; **162** Amtrak Train, Courtesy of Anaheim/Orange Country Visitor and Convention Bureau; **164/165** Surfer, Malibu, AA/M Jourdan; **166/167** International Aerospace Hall of Fame, San Diego, AA/M Jourdan; **168** Star of India, Maritime Museum, San Diego, AA/M Jourdan; **170/171** Gaslamp Quarter, San Diego, AA/M Jourdan; **172/173** San Diego Zoo, Courtesy of Anaheim/Orange Country Visitor and Convention Bureau; **174** Sequoia National Park, Brand X Pictures; **175** Sequoia National Park, Brand X Pictures; **176** Simi Valley Ronald W Reagan Presidential Library and Museum Air Force One Pavilion presidential aircraft, © Stephen Saks Photography/Alamy.

Every effort has been made to trace the copyright holders, and we apologise in advance for any unintentional omissions or errors. We would be pleased to apply any corrections in any following edition of this publication.

Sight locator index

This index relates to the maps on the covers. We have given map references to the main sights in the book. Some sights may not be plotted on the maps.